PREVIOUS BOOKS

How I Turn Ordinary Complaints into Thousands
of Dollars
A Great New Way to Make Money
How to Get the Upper Hand
How to Make Things Go Your Way
The Magic of Thinking Rich
How to Make Big Money in Low-priced Stocks
in the Coming Bull Market

SATISFACTION

☐ *The Ultimate Guide to*

GUARANTEED

Consumer Self-Defense □

Ralph Charell

LINDEN PRESS/SIMON & SCHUSTER

NEW YORK 1985

Published by Linden Press/Simon & Schuster
A Division of Simon & Schuster, Inc.
Simon & Schuster Building
Rockefeller Center
1230 Avenue of the Americas
New York, New York 10020
LINDEN PRESS/SIMON & SCHUSTER and colophon are trademarks of
Simon & Schuster, Inc.
Designed by Eve Kirch
Manufactured in the United States of America

10   9   8   7   6   5   4   3   2   1

Library of Congress Cataloging in Publication Data
Charell, Ralph.
    Satisfaction guaranteed.
    Includes index.
    1. Consumer protection—United States.   I. Title.
HC 110.C63C53   1985   381'.34'0973   85–197
ISBN: 0-671-49804-5

☐ Contents

In Search of Excellence   9

PART ONE
FROM MAD TO GLAD IN THE MARKETPLACE

Free to Choose   19
Great Expectations   22
Looking for Mr. Goodbar   25
Breaking the Sound Barrier   33
Dialing for Dollars   38
La Plume de ma Tante   42
Distinguishing Yourself   47
Getting to Yes   51
The Paper Chase   54
The Right Stuff   58
All in the Family   64
The Big Clock   69
Eliminate the Negative   74
Help!   78

For a Few Dollars More   85
Reasonableness   92

PART TWO
HOW TO DEAL WITH THE WORST OFFENDERS

Lawyers   101
Health Care   127
Travel   144
Stockbrokers   165
Home Improvements   185
Buying a Car: How to Drive a Bargain   205
Mail Order   226
How to Be Your Own Best Friend   243

Index   247

☐ In Search of Excellence

In *How I Turn Ordinary Complaints into Thousands of Dollars* (1973), I demonstrated that justified consumer complaints were more than simply sources of irritation and loss to be borne with discomfort. They were also items of value that could be converted with surprising ease to goods, services, belated civility, even deference—and cold cash. At the time the book was written, I had exchanged my own such ordinary complaints for more than $75,000 and *The Guinness Book of World Records* recognized me as "the world's most successful complainer."

In publicizing the book, I had the opportunity to speak with hundreds of people all over the country, in person and on call-in programs. People were not getting value for their money but they didn't know what to do about it. They felt taken advantage of and powerless and they seethed with anger. Some were amused by the lengths to which I had gone in handling my own consumer complaints. Others were heartened by the fact that a determined person of goodwill could go one-on-one with doctors, lawyers, bankers, brokers, hotels, restaurants, airlines, repair people, department stores

9

and other sellers who were clearly in the wrong and emerge with a favorable resolution of a tangled problem every time.

However, my recitations of personal success stories did not provide sufficient relief for others. I had been able to resolve my own justified complaints but there was a vast residue of unattended, legitimate complaints weighing on other people throughout the country. I was inundated with mail from unhappy consumers, and spent months responding to this outpouring in an effort to provide them some relief. I then set about the task of supplying specific antidotes to a number of problems we all commonly face as buyers of goods and services based on the conversations I'd had during the publicity tour, the available statistics, the mail and my own experiences. *How to Get the Upper Hand* (1978) resulted, forty-two chapters of solutions to problems commonly encountered in the marketplace.

Having thus presented compilations of both anecdotes and antidotes for the purpose of countering the rising tide of sloth, incompetence, rip-offs, arrogance, indifference and other peccadilloes commonly found among sellers, I thought my work in this field was done and I turned my attention to other pursuits. However, in recent years a number of significant shifts and changes have so altered the playing fields of the marketplaces in favor of sellers of services that a new game plan has become necessary before we are all marched off in lock step, like peevish lemmings, into querulous bankruptcy. A new, comprehensive and carefully drawn plan is needed to mark the faults, the falling-rock zones, the quagmires and the long, unrelieved stretches of quicksand in these marketplaces and to guide harried buyers through vast wastelands to the promised land, now only a deeply recessed tribal memory, the land of customer infallibility and complete buyer satisfaction.

In the several years since the publication of *How to Get the*

Upper Hand, an impressive network of governmental and quasi-governmental structures has been emplaced that spans the executive, judicial and legislative branches of our government at the federal, state and local levels. Consumer protection laws and agencies, supplemented by investigative and consumer reporters, citizen watchdogs, activists and a battalion of support troops have been put to work minding the store for the American consumer. This is all well and good with respect to products, but this mammoth effort has almost completely overlooked the much more important agenda of *services.* How much good does it do to enable Mrs. Smith and Mr. Jones to save a few dollars on generic drugs if the surgeon who operates on them does a mediocre job that permanently impairs their health when excellence would have restored it? What do you gain if the box of stationery you use in corresponding with your lawyer properly describes the quality of the paper when that highly paid advocate's mediocre services produce only a $25,000 settlement for you in a serious automobile accident case that would have been worth ten or twenty times that amount if the case had been handled with distinction?

The United States economy is now a predominantly service economy. More than half of the U.S. gross national product consists of services and the balance swings increasingly in this direction every day. It is a bitter irony that our society has committed tens of millions of dollars and other resources annually to provide what is commonly called "consumer protection," and yet almost nothing has been done to ensure that the consumer of services gets his/her money's worth.

You may inspect goods before you buy them. You may return them if you are dissatisfied. You are also protected by labeling. You can get a sea of materials specifications and other statistical data. Government and independent laboratories test the product. Ratings services evaluate them. Additional large sums are committed to product research by private industry, governmental agencies and consumer-oriented organizations. Most of these data are available to you before you buy.

However, little or nothing is spent evaluating most of the important services you buy. If you want to bet $2.00 on a horse, for a few extra pennies you may obtain his or her pedigree and lifetime track record, replete with exact performance times under specified track conditions. If you want to hazard your life on a surgeon or your fortune on a lawyer, you cannot obtain equivalent data about the practitioner's past performance. There is no rating system for your doctor or lawyer or surgeon or stockbroker or barber or therapist.

Nor do you have the ordinary guidepost of price to help you evaluate services. Prices vary by hundreds, even thousands of percents, and comparison is difficult because there are usually so many variables in each equation. You may visit a doctor for $10.00 or pay $200 to have a different physician in the same city examine the same complaint. You may have your income tax figured for $20 or pay one or two dozen times as much, your hair cut for $3.00 or $50, and the cost of a lawyer's time varies as widely. However, you may easily be paying top dollar not only for a poor result but also for a poor practitioner. There is simply no direct relationship between the price of services and their value.

You may hold a toaster in your hands and examine it before you buy it. Not so with services. The commitment to pay for services is usually made before you are sure of what you will be receiving. Furthermore, if you buy a toaster and it doesn't toast, it's not too difficult to exchange it for one that does work. You can't take back a ruined vacation or a bad lawsuit or a surgical operation that didn't "work." Your losses may be a hundred or a thousand times greater than those associated with a defective toaster, yet you ordinarily have no remedy. There is a protective barrier wider than Moon River surrounding and insulating the mediocre practitioner from a successful malpractice suit. Mediocrity is not actionable, regardless of your loss and the fact that excellence would have prevailed for you. Sadly, excellence is an endangered species, bordering on extinction.

Unfortunate in the extreme, there is an almost total lack of information about how to be a satisfied buyer of services in this, the largest service economy in the history of the world. Why do so many people repeatedly suffer the pain of paying high prices for personal services only to be handed the "one size that fits all" kind of service that is designed to fit nobody well? In short, all too often you don't know what you're paying for, you have no set of specifications, no warranty and no recourse when you don't get what you thought you were buying. As its main order of business, then, *Satisfaction Guaranteed* addresses the buyer's problems and concerns with respect to a number of typical purchases that, in the aggregate, cost the American consumer more than a trillion dollars annually and are, at the same time, the leading causes of buyer dissatisfactions and complaints.

In addition, the book spells out in detail how to go from mad to glad in the marketplace and presents my world championship complaints system, the complete outfit of tactics, techniques, preventives and cures for resolving any and all justified consumer complaints in your favor. For the first time, the entire system is set forth and illustrated clearly.

In the several years since the publication of *How to Get the Upper Hand,* the other side has had ample time to adjust to the fixed defenses of specific antidotes. A hardier, more virulent strain of wrongdoer now slyly offers to do business with us. This malevolent mutant, characterized by an ever-thickening carapace and an almost total disregard for quid pro quo, faces unwary buyers in stores, showrooms, offices and other marketplace sites throughout the country. The consequences of these thousands of daily overmatches are all too well documented and other, less deviant sellers have been attracted by the easy pickings of the mutants. As the ethics of the marketplace disintegrate, our citizenry is being commercially mugged not only by mutants or by otherwise normal men and women operating under extreme circumstances. These outrages are being perpetrated daily and routinely by ordinary people in the most ordinary of circumstances.

Even as sellers are taking advantage of buyers individually and in clusters, other market forces are working toward the same end. Much has been written about the so-called market mechanism, a kind of giant, invisible hand that allegedly moves in mysterious ways to correct imbalances and improprieties and restore fair and orderly markets. I have much respect for the market mechanism, but the law of supply and demand on which it is based, and which balanced buyers and sellers for centuries, has been compromised. The equation has become distorted and is in considerable danger of being destroyed.

For decades a raging inflation fueled by massive increases in the money supply strengthened the sell side at the expense of the buyer. The effect on prices is clear. A $3.00 tie, now "designer," costs $27.50. A $6.00 shirt is $59.95. Dinner for two at a three-star restaurant is out of reach for most people and it costs almost as much (in pretax earnings) to educate your offspring as it took our forbears to retire in comfort in a house of their own.

In good economic times, goods and services, not cash, rule the marketplace. Sellers are in the saddle and they ride roughshod over buyers. Standards of performance, of ethics, of quality control, productivity and value tend to crumble and give way. In bad times, you take what you can get if you have anything left to pay for it.

The invisible hand no longer quietly guides each transaction. It is stealthily rummaging in your pocket or purse or adding weight to the seller's scales with a leaden thumb. Unchecked and grown brazen, the hand is often disconnected from reason and equity. A graceless shove from behind, an insolent slap in the face, emboldened, the hand may even occasionally find its way to your throat. Visible at times, the hand may direct unsuspecting traffic toward a new and intricate maze, a shiny squirrel cage or a fresh roll of sticky red tape—and all of these transgressions are proliferating like paramecia in a petri dish.

Buying something, which used to be an enjoyable, even exhilarating exchange of values, has become considerably less pleasurable. The customer, no longer always right, is too often either barely tolerated, treated with open hostility or simply ripped off, on the one hand, or is kept waiting in a kind of gigantic post office in which all of the machinery is out of order and the only window open is staffed by a civil servant whose movements are phlegmatic.

Only a systematic approach to all of the many seller excesses can provide sufficient flexibility for complete relief and protection. The system's grid must be broad enough to encompass all of the problems with which we are all too familiar and the mesh fine enough to prevent any mutants and their many impersonators from slipping through the cracks. The complete method proposed in these pages is legal, socially acceptable and completely within the system. The applications are simple, effective, economical and virtually unlimited. The complete complaints system utilizes a repertoire of behaviors to give you total satisfaction should an occasional misguided seller stray too far beyond the bounds of propriety when you are on the opposite side of the transaction.

Like a well-matched set of golf clubs, each of the tools in the system is designed for a specific function and they work best in concert. A little practice with all of the clubs in the bag will give you the flexibility to master any course, regardless of the hazards you may encounter on your way. You will then be able to sally forth confidently and lightheartedly into any marketplace no longer fair prey, no longer routinely subjected to short weight or squelched self-esteem, but safe, secure and serene in the knowledge that you can create good results through your own efforts, at will. Any obstacles you may encounter from time to time will merely be circumstances to be challenged and changed. Problems and difficulties in the marketplace will only be thinly disguised opportunities easily unmasked and converted to value received and complete satisfaction.

Thus, mediocrity and random results will be banished from your life and in their place will be an abundance of excellence, of high-quality goods and services beautifully and skillfully designed for the uses you intend. As a bonus, as you gain control over your purchases you will also find yourself paying less, getting more and being treated better than ever. Should an occasional contretemps arise and not resolve itself favorably on request, your mental caddy need only reach into the complete complaints golf bag for the proper club with which to provide quick relief. In sum, this is the promise and the meaning of *Satisfaction Guaranteed*.

☐ PART ONE

*From Mad to Glad
in the Marketplace*

□

The objective of Part One of Satisfaction Guaranteed *is to provide both a safety net to cushion the impact when mutants and other like-minded sellers upset your balance in the marketplace and a complete armamentarium with which to correct such occasional imbalances. In contesting these affronts, the more parts of the outcome you can control, the more control you have over the final disposition of the matter at hand. Your command of the situation is governed by decisions and choices you make in securing your objectives. To help you obtain the blessed relief often reserved for the third act, while sparing you the agonies of the second, I've looked back over twenty years of my own successes in creating turnabouts and fair play for myself as a buyer and distilled the results into a complete method anybody can use.*

□

☐ Free to Choose

Nettlesome sellers and their unwelcome fallout abound in the marketplace and you may expect to encounter your share. However, as you develop confidence in your ability to convert bad marketplace experiences to happy endings, you will probably notice a change in your behavior. Those given to taking up the cudgels at every real or imagined slight will no longer feel called upon to do so. Secure in their own power, like black belt karate players, they will be able to walk away from many altercations with undiminished dignity. The long-suffering souls who were too timid or unsure ever to complain will also move toward the norm and discover their newly freed, inner voices.

When to go to the mat is a personal choice and reasonable people may differ about whether to accept a given challenge. What engages me in this or that imbroglio may not have the same effect on you, and vice versa. Nevertheless, I have found the following guidelines useful in making these decisions.

First, it is important to realize that you have a choice. It isn't always necessary to complain and seek redress for the slightest miscue. Your ability to handle anything that may arise gives you the freedom to stop acting automatically and exercise true choices.

Some marketplace wrongs are so minor and their effects so minimal that they may be overlooked. Why complain when there's only a small upside potential? In the interest of charity and harmony and of getting on with your life, it's best to keep your powder dry for much bigger game.

Other substandard performances turned in by sellers are so close to being minimally acceptable that you can be magnanimous and give the other side the benefit of the doubt. I don't pursue 55/45 situations or other instances where I have a small preponderance of equity in my favor. Absent other negative factors, such as bad intent, for example, I prefer to give the other side much latitude in which to ply their trade with immunity. Live and let live. My circuits become overloaded only in much more clear-cut cases of wrongdoing. Then, too, many close cases, if contested, may entail large or total losses for the seller and only trivial gains for me. It would be unseemly to oblige the other side to absorb the entire loss when the deficit I face is so disproportionately small.

I also recommend against your direct, unrepresented involvement in cases that involve a potentially large downside personal risk. We're in this game for profits, not losses. Not everybody you do business with is a levelheaded, legitimate business or professional person. Some sellers are crazed or criminal and besting them *mano-a-mano* may not end the matter. You may face retaliation that jeopardizes you in unacceptable ways.

Such bizarre continuations are relatively rare and they usually involve unsupervised individuals, independent contractors (especially those who work with their hands), proprietors of small businesses and the self-employed. Large, publicly traded companies in this country don't often keep such unstable employees on their payrolls, nor are those who work for major companies likely to take being bested personally. However, the list of situations in which clinically significant pathology may be encountered, while small, is growing. Always err on the side of prudence. When in doubt, pass.

Having thus winnowed out of your life the marginal cases, those involving the potentially small upside return or the big downside risk, the residue will be surprisingly large. Incompetence is a growth industry and carelessness and procrastination can now be transmitted genetically. Only the further rigorous application of the selectivity principle can keep your docket manageable.

Look for the flagrant cases. A slight lack of care may be overlooked, but reckless disregard or gross negligence is a different matter. Bad intent on the seller's part is never a mitigating factor. The size and scale of the transaction are also parts of the equation, as are the effects of a given wrong on you and those for whom you speak. In general, you will be extremely well served if you don't act hastily or intemperately, learn to win the disputes you consider important and don't give the others any energy.

☐ Great Expectations

The first step in resolving a selected consumer complaint to your satisfaction is to decide what would make you whole and happy. Keep your expectations high. Statistically, the most significant difference between people who do well in these situations and those who don't is that the former expect to do well. High expectations are invariably communicated to the other side and affect the resolution process. No matter how legitimate your claim may be, no seller gives you more than you ask for in resolving a dispute.

Take the case of a small insurance claim. The adjuster is so used to hearing inflated claims, disbelief at any insured's initial estimate comes leaping to mind automatically. The adjuster won't feel comfortable unless the original demand is pared down. Hence, the ritual calls for your opening offer to be on the high side. It's how you play the game that determines whether you win or lose. The honest claimant who states what he/she believes is a reasonable outcome as the original estimate receives much less than the honest claimant who begins higher. The choice is yours.

Adjuster: Assuming that everything else is in order, how much are we talking about here?

You (refusing to observe, or ignorant of, the ritual): About $750.

The adjuster acts out the primary symptoms of angina or, if he/she is more verbal, expresses shocked disbelief.

Adjuster: What! I was thinking we could close it out for $250, maybe $300 tops.

The rest is predictable. You'll be lucky to walk away with $500 or you will reach an impasse. If you'd played the hand by the book, the outcome would have been different.

Adjuster: . . . how much are we talking about here?

You (respecting the ritual): Well, it cost us $1,800 and it's practically new. I would say at *least* twelve, thirteen hundred.

The primary angina symptoms or the exclamation follows on cue. However, the number quoted by the adjuster as his/her first offer won't be quite as off the mark. It'll be kicked up to three, four hundred. You and the adjuster will have a cup of coffee or a soft drink, the adjuster will feel good about paring down your claim and it's a fast wrap because you were willing to follow the script and come in high, as expected. This little scene will play itself out to about the $750 you had in mind in the first place.

Normally, in a real life situation you should not state your settlement price until much later in the play of the hand, after you've done some further positioning (as will be outlined later). What's more, you should state your price only when asked by somebody who can pay it. When the resolution process has matured to the point of closing, somebody with closing authority for the other side will often ask you what you want. This is a good sign. You must be prepared to field this question cleanly with a specific answer on the high side. If you fail to reply with a specific answer, you will put the other person off and upset the delicate timing of the close. Deciding on your objective in advance and keeping your expectations high will also guide you past gatekeepers who lack the authority to satisfy your demands (but who may try to obstruct your progress) to those who can give you what you want.

☐ Looking for Mr. Goodbar

In this game, as in tennis, you don't have to win every point to win every match. In fact, you have to win only a single key point to win each match. Moreover, you may even lose this key point several times before you finally win it and end the match. Thus, in virtually every contest, you're in a situation in which it's heads you win and tails it doesn't count. This overwhelming advantage allows your skills to beat the other side's much greater size and weight consistently. Secure in this knowledge, you may remain calm and confident. You no longer have to worry about every little lob or drop shot or about how much top spin the other side may have put on some insignificant return.

The key to winning each match is to reach a person who has the ability and the authority to give you what you want and to motivate him or her to do so. In most of the situations you choose to complain about, a number of people can and will help you and many more can't or won't. The crucial idea is to seek out the former and avoid the latter. If you can control who pays you, you can influence what you get. This is not so difficult as it may seem.

As a general rule, follow the established procedures in routine situations. If you've been billed the wrong amount on a department-store charge account, give customer service or the billing department the first opportunity to correct the error. These people are not only familiar with this everyday occurrence and know how to correct it, but the remedy you seek (adjusting your account) is also routine and entirely within their competence and jurisdiction.

However, if the situation is more complicated or the result you want to accomplish unusual (or even unprecedented), the entry level for discussion will have to be higher, where authority and ability are less limited. Some have suggested that all problems, big and small, routine as well as unusual, be directed to the chief executive officer of the company. This is a tactical error to be avoided.

First, you are unlikely to reach this lofty executive, as trained, tested and reliable personnel are emplaced to prevent precisely these kinds of direct contacts. Your call or letter will be intercepted and rerouted to much lower-level personnel not of your own choosing. You will have lost time and, more important, control of the spigot whence your compensation issues. Furthermore, if you begin at the top and actually reach somebody in charge, an unfavorable decision will create an adverse record that is likely to follow your appeal, to your detriment. It is much harder to reverse a top-level decision against you than it is to win at a lower level.

On the other hand, if you initiate your complaint more carefully and control its rerouting yourself, even if your efforts are not immediately availing, you have room in which to maneuver at higher levels without any decision against you on the record, as illustrated below. As you move upward, you will also be developing information, perhaps admissions against the seller's interests and other positional advantages you may later convert to a win, whereas if you begin at or near the top you will not have an opportunity to gain these benefits. Therefore, take your complaint to somebody who has the authority and the ability to help you but allow room for appeals to higher authority within the organization if you're not satisfied.

I made the point earlier that there are usually several people on the other side who can give you what you want but they are not equally disposed to do so. Like the members of any other group, they have their individual differences, their quirks and idiosyncracies. Some service people who listen to long, irate recitations of alleged company errors and omissions all day are at the point of overload when you call. Others may defend themselves from premature burnout by putting problems that legitimately need their attention out of sight and mind in wastebaskets, under rugs, behind radiators or in drain spouts.

You can avoid these non-helpers if you learn to set your initial contact with them in a way that indicates whether you have reached such an obstructionist or whether you are speaking with a genuinely service-oriented person *before* you present the problem to be solved or create a written record. The telephone is not only more efficient than a letter or a personal visit, it also gives you enormous access to many people and lots of control. With a little sensitivity you can "read" the other person, and if you've reached a non-helper, end the call before an adverse decision is recorded and move on to somebody else.

As you experience a range of responses from personnel speaking for the seller, you will develop an almost uncanny ability to pick up even subtle differences in voice tones and separate yourself from those who cannot or will not help you while you concentrate your efforts on those who can and will. You may already have developed this skill if you are a careful listener.

Telephone, identify yourself and ask for the other's name. Your voice should be pleasant and without a trace of rancor. "My name is Suzanne Hall. Who is this, please?" Some people give their names at once when they pick up a telephone. The response to these people, instead of the question suggested, should be "I'm sorry. I didn't get your name." The idea is to get the other person to speak in a way that quickly reveals his/her attitude toward your inquiry. You won't have any visual cues to guide your decision so pay particular attention to what you hear. A clear, direct answer that unhesitatingly identifies the other person is good. If it is followed by "What may I do for you?" or "How may I help you?" it is even better.

If, however, you don't get a direct answer or there is too long a pause, even before the matter to be discussed has been put on the table, you would be unwise to continue the discussion. Similarly, the answer "What's your problem?" or its equivalent in lieu of the name indicates that you are being viewed as the enemy and that you have reached someone insufficiently service-oriented.

Your best response to an unsatisfactory answer at this early stage is to end the conversation in a way that will not linger in the other person's memory or impel him or her to create a written record. You're not interested in winning two out of three falls. You want to obtain a good result as quickly and easily as possible and you want to avoid the burden of reversing an unfavorable decision. "I'm very sorry. Something just came up. (You bet it did.) I have to go. Excuse me. Good-bye." Try again later.

If you're dealing with a medium-sized, or bigger, company, it's a piece of cake. Call the company switchboard and, in a voice resonating with goodwill, say, "Let me speak with the chief operator (or supervisor), please." As nothing untoward has occurred prior to your asking to speak with the chief operator or supervisor and as your voice tone is clear and upbeat, you should be put through at once.

On the rare occasion when the response is "What is this in reference to?" or "Maybe I can help you," your reply is simple. "This is a fairly complicated matter and I need to speak with the chief (supervisor)." Switchboard operators don't want to hear your "complicated matter," much less discuss it or try to resolve it, so your call will almost undoubtedly be passed along.

You've been pleasant but distant. You've used few words, creating an implacable facade that gives the other no purchase, no opening. There's little else to be done, except by the more seriously aberrant employees, than to transfer your call as requested.

"This is the chief operator."

"Thank you. We've been buying at Higginbottom's for many years. My name is Claudia Hanes. May I ask your name?"

You've acknowledged the chief's willingness to take the call by thanking him/her. Your tone is pleasant. You've established yourself as a good customer of long standing. Your use of the first person plural adds a little weight. You've identified yourself, adding a measure of credibility and goodwill by giving your name first and by including your first name. You've asked for the chief's name. You prefer not to deal anonymously as accountability in the form of the other's name will encourage a little better effort.

If you get anything less than a name without any pause, you probably have *not* reached the chief or the supervisor. If you get a name after a pause, respond by asking, "Am I speaking with the chief operator (or supervisor), Mr./Ms.

So-and-So?" Say this calmly and say nothing more. If there is no immediate answer, or if the other person falters or admits he/she is not the chief operator (or supervisor), ask, "Is the chief operator (or supervisor) there *now?*" If this doesn't produce the desired result, after a pause, ask, "What is the chief's name?" After you get this name, calmly say, "Let me speak with Mr./Ms. Whatever," playing the name back exactly as you heard it pronounced.

"This is Mrs. Parker." The chief operator (or supervisor) has now identified herself.

"Mrs. Parker, I'm (or we're) having a problem about a toaster. Who is the *best* person in the store to *help* us?"

The person you spoke with initially has already told the chief operator this is a complicated problem. Don't repeat. Don't go into detail. Switchboards reward brevity and obstruct verbosity. Summarize wherever possible but answer direct questions. Chief operators are not linguistics professors but brevity and the right choice of words, even if subtle, work in your favor. "Am having" implies a certain temporariness. You've also asked for the *best* person to *help* with a toaster problem. This implies that you know that more than one person might take your call, and by emphasizing the word "help" you're focusing the chief on what you want: a helper, not some pompous executive or assistant who will obstruct your purpose. You also know that chief operators know more about the table of organization of the company they work for than the vice president in charge of office paintings, as it takes several years to become a chief operator and knowing who's who and how the firm is connected is the essence of the job.

"That would be the small-appliance department."

"Who would be the *best* person in the small-appliance department, Mrs. Parker?"

By repeating her words as much as possible ("would be,"

"the small-appliance department"), you're getting into synchronization with her speech patterns. This promotes instant rapport and cooperation. You've also repeated her name, always good, as it adds a note of personal recognition and a small handle of control.

"Mr. Longo."

"Mr. Longo. Thank you very much, Mrs. Parker. I appreciate your help. One last question. To whom does Mr. Longo report?"

You've acknowledged her, played back the name of Mr. Longo, thanked her and let her know there's only one more answer needed to end the conversation, all of which motivates your receiving the answer you seek.

"Mrs. Keller."

"Mrs. Keller. Much obliged. Thank you again, very much, Mrs. Parker."

Let's pause here and review the bidding. You have a justified complaint about goods or services that meets your selectivity criteria. You have a good idea of what you want by way of recompense and your expectations are high. You realize you'll probably need to reach at least middle management to find the combination of sufficient authority and ability to give you what you have in mind. You know that several company employees can deliver your objective and many can't or won't. You've avoided the creation of an adverse record, finessing the burden of having to get it overruled.

You enlisted the assistance of the seller's chief operator or switchboard supervisor to guide your complaint to a deliverer. This source not only has the information you want but is also relatively disinterested in the outcome. The matter will be decided elsewhere, far from the company switchboard, and the switchboard personnel aren't even aware of the details of the matter. There's nothing with which to become emotionally involved if you've been courteous. The chief is about as neutral as an elevator operator transporting other, less knowledgeable, complainers to the customer service department. It is reasonable to expect that this guidance will take you far beyond the usual traffic patterns with its snarls, slippery shoulders and dead ends.

You have separated yourself from the mass of legitimate complainers who will never be satisfied. This is not meant to imply that American business wants to cheat you, take advantage of you or not give you your due, but a combination of factors is at work to keep you from your full remedy if you take the usual route. Not all employees perform well at the job they are paid to do. In addition, the authority to give away company money or other assets is extremely limited and the few who have it are difficult to reach, raising the cost of complaining and discouraging many from so doing. The other side knows that the more obstacles and burdens they impose on the complaining customer, the fewer "make-goods" the company will have to write off.

So much the more so is this the case when what you want is unusual. In any event, and for whatever combination of reasons companies cite, a multitude of legitimately aggrieved customers bleat themselves hoarse annually or consume a small forest with long, detailed complaint letters, to no avail.

On the other hand, via the process suggested, in a single telephone call made in a couple of minutes of your downtime and over toll-free or company tie lines wherever possible, you've covered a great deal of ground. You have the name of somebody your unpaid expert thinks is the best person to help you in the specific area of your complaint and you also know the name of his/her boss. All that now remains is to reach and motivate Mr. Longo in this case, or, generically, Mr./Ms. Big.

☐ Breaking the Sound Barrier

It's not easy to reach Mr. or Ms. Big. Whenever you call, you are likely to be told by a secretary, subordinate or other gatekeeper that Big is not at the desk. Big is always in a meeting on another floor or he's inspecting a plant in Suriname. She's in an airplane over Istanbul or working at home, having left strict orders not to be disturbed. Sometimes, if you're lucky you may miss him or her narrowly: "He's just gone to lunch" or "She's getting into the elevator right now, en route to the airport." You try again and again, while your days turn to nights, your mind to jelly. You are invariably turned away and finally give up. Score another save for the goalies and gatekeepers, another zero for the customer.

Much of what you've been told, of course, is nonsense. Often, Mr. Big was actually in his office when you called, perhaps struggling with the crossword puzzle with his feet up on the desk or gossiping with another busy executive down the hall. Ms. Big may have been staring at her Rolodex trying to figure out what to have for lunch and where and with whom to have it.

I devised a simple technique with which to break this

sound barrier several years ago and described it in *How to Get the Upper Hand.* Here it is, updated and refined. Call at a time you would normally expect to find Big at the desk, say about 11:30 A.M. or 4:30 P.M. Many executives set aside these times for making and taking calls and it's much easier to get through. Make your call person-to-person. Even a *local* call may be made person-to-person by dialing "O" for operator, then the area code and the number.

For a slight extra charge (if you are able to reach this elusive personage; otherwise, there is no charge at all) you get a number of advantages. First, you increase your importance, as person-to-person calls are usually long-distance. Second, a paid person-to-person call is almost irresistible if the called party is available. Third, you enlist the services of an official-sounding telephone company operator to announce your call and act as a buffer between you and Big's subordinate.

When the operator tells Big's assistant or secretary that you are calling Big, the subordinate has to make a decision based on insufficient information. If you had placed the call directly, you would have been subjected to the usual questioning. "What is this in reference to?" or "Does he/she know what this is about?" No doubt you would have been turned away if you failed to voice the password.

You finesse this nonsense by interposing a third party. The underling can hardly question the operator and if you simply remain silent if any such questions are put, the decision not to prevent your apparent long-distance call from getting through to Big is likely. If, however, the secretary or assistant balks at this by insisting on more information as to the nature of the call or informs the operator that Big is not available at the moment, you immediately enter the conversation and quickly take charge:

"This is a rather simple matter that Mr. Big can easily handle. However, if he is unavailable right now, would you kindly transfer this call to Mr. *Bigger!*"

Bigger, of course, is Big's boss. You've gotten Big's name and that of his boss from the chief switchboard operator or supervisor, as previously suggested. Mentioning Big's boss in this way requires the subordinate to make another decision quickly. Secretaries and assistants are aware that their boss doesn't want waves made in his/her direction from above in the corporate hierarchy for any reason—ever. Big will surely not want to have his/her boss disturbed about a routine matter Big sought to avoid, one that you have already characterized as rather simple and easily handled by Big.

The net result is that if Big is actually at the desk, the call is likely to be put through without further evasion. "Oh, he's just rounding the corridor now, Ms. Goodperson." Of course. He just dropped out of the skies over Istanbul and fell to earth at his desk.

When Big picks up the call, never rub it in by saying "I thought the secretary said you weren't in." The idea is for Big to *want* to help you but not to bludgeon him or her and thus induce resistance or, equally unproductive, have him/her give you apparent agreement followed by nonperformance.

If Big is, in fact, not in, the subordinate, out of loyalty to Big and fear of possible recriminations later, will be reluctant to transfer the call to Big's boss. The likely response in that case is "Mr. Big will be back in his office in about twenty minutes and he will return your call at that time." If yours is actually a long-distance call, you may now tighten the reins a bit. "I can be reached at the following number for the next half hour or so. If I don't hear from him by then, I'll call Mr. Bigger directly."

If, however, your call was a local one, you don't want to reveal this fact and ruin the illusion. "I'm going to be in and out and don't want to miss Mr. Big *again*. I'll call back in half an hour and if he's still unavailable, I'll call Mr. Bigger directly." This keeps the pot boiling, maintaining the pressure on Big. When you call back later, do so with the operator's assistance again. It increases your apparent investment and creates a better climate for resolution.

Whether you speak with Big at once or later the same day, you have the ear of somebody with the ability and authority to give you what you want and you've motivated him to do so because Big knows that unless you're pleased, there's an excellent chance that Bigger will be contacted, creating the risk that Bigger will also hear how Big has been ducking a good customer's many attempts to resolve a justified complaint.

For best results, when you reach Big, put it to him early on, gently and without rancor, that you've been given something of a runaround. "I've had a rather trying time reaching you, Mr. Big, and nobody in your office has ever returned a single one of my calls until today. Why would management want to mistreat its best customers?"

Big will assure you it's not their policy to do so, trying to sidestep the element of personal jeopardy you have casually introduced onto the field of play. Big would prefer that Bigger not learn of his chronic unavailability, his lack of ordinary courtesy and his unsympathetic handling of a good customer's legitimate complaint. This strengthens your position and should bolster the bottom line for you.

Speaking of which, you may be happily surprised to learn how much of the company's assets Big is willing to part with, and how speedily he can get them delivered to you. These assets, after all, are not Big's. They belong to the stockholders in the typical case and the difference on the corporate balance sheet between a poor result for you and an excellent one is minuscule from Big's point of view. It's a bargain if it avoids even the slightest personal jeopardy.

☐ Dialing for Dollars

I made the point earlier that you don't have to win every point in this game to win every match. All that is necessary is to win the one key point that ends the match, and you may even lose this key point several times before you finally win it and end the match to your complete satisfaction. The strategy in handling this advantage is to arrange matters so that the other side has to defend several match points, any one of which, if lost, means a desirable resolution of the matter for you. The more match points the other side must defend, the more chances you have to win the match.

The telephone is a real equalizer in this game. It's a low-risk opportunity, it's convenient, inexpensive and often brings results out of all proportion to the time and effort required. However, the greater the value of your objective, the fewer people in the seller's organization have the authority to give it to you and the higher in the hierarchy you will have to reach. It's amazing how few people even in a major corporation can authorize a check for as little as $25.

Therefore, if some employee with an important-sounding title pooh-poohs your complaint, don't ever be a lemming and doubt its validity or propriety. Take this reaction as a sign the person thus expressing his/her dubiety lacks the authority to give you what you want and deserve as well as the candor to admit it. Press on.

In a case in point, I had been buying stationery from the same company for many years. I'd originally had a die struck by the company of my name and address. This was engraved on the back flap of the envelope but only the name was engraved on the letter paper, a common arrangement. When one of my reorders of a hundred letter sheets arrived, there seemed to be an overcharge. I called to ask about it and was told this was the customary "omit" charge.

"Do you mean I've been charged $15 per hundred to have my address omitted from the letter sheets?"

I took the sneering condescension in the tone of the reply as an unmistakable sign of lack of authority. It was two full levels higher that I reached somebody who attempted to explain the company's policy. It seems that there is a little extra work involved in omitting the address when stamping the letter paper, hence the charge.

"Then why didn't we cut another die with only the name?" I asked.

"We could do that."

"For how much?"

"That would be $22."

"It was probably more like $10 when I ordered the original die. If anybody had ever informed me that you charged $15 per hundred sheets to omit my address from the letter papers, I certainly would have ordered the other die. I also think there *must* be some regulation prohibiting charging a customer in this way without itemizing the charge so that it's impossible to know what you're paying for. I hope you don't mind my pointing this out."

"What do you want?"

"I won't put you to the trouble of repaying me for all the past omit charges but I certainly think we should at least reverse this charge on the current bill and order a die struck with only the name at no additional charge."

"We could do that."

There's some good technique in this little example. First, I wasn't put off at all when the first two levels of authority sneered at my complaint, nor did I give it more than about the three or four minutes it deserved. Second, my objective was clear. I wanted the matter to be resolved permanently and the current charge removed. My voice tone was clear, strong, upbeat and not overbearing. Think Charleton Heston or Jane Fonda. I finessed the people who couldn't or wouldn't help me without creating any adverse record and moved upward to higher authority with the help of the company switchboard. I summarized the matter and was courteous.

I also pointed out that there *must* (a useful word) be some regulation prohibiting what had been done. This is a nice touch as it takes advantage of the huge apparatus of departments of consumer affairs and their counterparts without even having to take the time to enlist their help. It invokes outside authority and introduces jeopardy, but obliquely, without citing any specific regulation and without raising the temperature of the conversation. This is important when dealing with high-level executives. They don't like to be threatened head-on, but this was indirect.

Then, when I heard the signal that we were getting to the bottom line—"What do you want?"—I was ready to scoop up the ball cleanly and make the putout. I also made it a little easier to accept what I had in mind by mentioning that I didn't intend to put them "to the trouble" (note no mention of money here; it's often best not to be too crass with higher management personnel) of repaying past omit charges. Note also the words "certainly" and "at least." This added some weight to the request and ended the matter. It's such a simple presentation, it can hardly fail, and I hasten to add that had the situation been reversed, I would have been happy to close it out the same way. What's unfortunate is that so many people don't make the effort to turn these situations about, and when they do, they are often so easily sidestepped by an underling.

A couple of caveats. The people at the other end of the telephone who can resolve your complaints are experienced at reading voice tones. Don't posture, professing to know much more than you do about their operation. Don't do your John Houseman impression. That's very effective if you're a professor and you have a captive audience of students, but you've got nothing in the bank to draw on in these encounters. By the same token, you're not Olive Oyl either. "Poor me" is one of the surest turn-offs in the book. Only the fire department handles limp bodies in the line of duty.

If you don't get the results you want at once, hang up and dial again. Pretty soon, if you observe good practice, you'll be able to reach out and touch someone whenever you like for whatever's reasonable.

☐ La Plume de ma Tante

Remember this scene in the jungle pictures of the 1940s? The intrepid adventurer, his sidekick, the beautiful heroine and her father have been captured by cannibals. A huge cauldron is being heated and the bound prisoners are shortly to be boiled alive. Suddenly, the hero stares up at the sky, says a few nonsense syllables and an eclipse of the sun (or moon) commences. Whereupon the natives throw down their spears, unbind their captives and prostrate themselves before their new god.

A variation on this theme may be profitably applied to your excursions to the land of buy and sell, a place still marked by knowledgeable cartographers as wild terrain on the edges of the world "where monsters be." The idea is to select words and phrases so emotionally charged that the desired action is reflexive. Delivered with a little insight and skill—how you say the words can be as decisive as what you say—you can evoke the conditioned reflex with astonishing ease and speed.

There is enormous power to influence the behavior of other people contained in the right handy words or phrases.

You simply make use of what is already in the mind of the person you're seeking to influence. All the preliminary work has been done. Everything is wired in place. All you have to do is press the right button.

I began to think about this more than a decade ago, as some readers may recall from one of my earlier books. I had been a guest on an early morning network television program and, as I was leaving the studio, a call came in from a woman in Georgia who'd been watching the program. She wanted to know whether I could help her with a serious problem.

She'd been hospitalized with a kidney ailment and after a couple of cursory, negative tests she'd been discharged but still felt terrible. What should she do? I was touched by her plight and by the fact that she was calling a total stranger long-distance on the chance that I could somehow be of help. She sounded upset and unhappy and I wished I could say some magic words to set things right for her, but what magic could I summon? Suddenly, I had an idea.

"What's the name of the governor of Georgia?"

"Carter. Jimmy Carter."

"Carter's too common a name for what I have in mind. Let's try Senator Stennis. You might consider this. Go to a different hospital. When you sign in, use the name Stennis as your middle name, as if it's a family name. Everybody will know that name and when they ask you if you're related to Senator Stennis, just say that you don't want *any* special treatment because of your family connections."

What else would work as well? Obviously, the word "doctor" in a hospital. What about the word "lawyer"? Could that word, added to a kettle about to boil over, suddenly cool it to room temperature? Say you're headed for an impasse with somebody who can deliver your objective and you pull out this one: "You know, Mr. Grimm, you're talking to a very angry attorney." There seems to be an implied threat here. You haven't said that this company is one pip away from being slapped with a lawsuit if you're not satisfied and that it's child's play for you to do this because you, yourself, are a lawyer—but it's hanging in the air. Why not take the other road, reason together and resolve the dispute? Would you want to be the cause of a major lawsuit for your company because you failed to handle a customer's justified complaint?

Well, if the judicious invocations of the words "doctor" and "lawyer" are so effective, what might be effective in disputes with doctors and lawyers themselves? Why the county bar association or medical society! Reference to these and other licensing bodies, regulatory agencies and the like are, indeed, effective.

Our cat had been an outpatient in an experimental program at Memorial Sloan-Kettering Hospital in New York City. The doctors there had cured his lymphosarcoma and his feline leukemia virus had been in remission for a couple of years. However, he had glaucoma in one eye, which was said to be incurable, but we wondered whether we could help him overcome this disease, too.

My wife called a fairly well-known local veterinarian, explained that the glaucoma had been diagnosed by a veterinarian as well as an M.D. at the hospital and asked whether the vet could help. She was given an appointment. When we arrived, the vet looked at the cat for about two minutes, introduced us to the D.V.M. who owned the facility and suggested that we see a specialist later in the day. It cost $30 for this "examination" and it would be an additional $50 to see the specialist on the premises or somewhat less if we chose to see the latter at a nearby clinic, where he also worked.

I was asked to pay the $30 at once. There were other ill animals as well as our own on the premises and I didn't want to create any stress for them so I wrote out a check, but I didn't like the way we or our cat had been treated. When we got home, I called the Veterinary Medical Association of New York City, outlined the facts and asked how to process a complaint. I was told to address the complaint to their Grievance and Ethics Committee. "Perhaps I should speak with the vet in charge before making a formal complaint," I suggested. The secretary thought that was a good idea.

I then called the benefactor-entrepreneur who ran the animal facility. To protect the guilty, let's call him Dr. D. Rap Dade.

"My name is Charell," I told Dr. Dade. "I spoke with the Veterinary Medical Association after our visit this morning and they thought it would be a good idea to speak with you before processing a complaint with the Grievance and Ethics Committee."

Dr. Dade was interested at once. I pointed out that the cat had been properly diagnosed by a D.V.M. and an M.D. and that we'd come in not for a diagnosis or referral but for treatment, as had been explained before the appointment was scheduled. It was preposterous and improper to pay somebody $30 for telling us to come back later and pay somebody else $50 to treat him.

"I think you should also know that the cat didn't enjoy being put into a carrier for a wasted round trip. I hope other animals will be spared this sort of needless trauma."

Dr. D. Rap Dade conceded there was some merit to what he called my "point of view" and suggested tearing up my check. That ended the matter.

There are a number of other effective words and phrases that make use of information already stored in the seller's mental cupboard. Sometimes, when the other side gets a little overbearing, I restructure the conversation with this positioner:

Overbearing Other Side: . . . and blah-blah-blah, etc., and so forth, and you're going to have to put all the facts in writing and we'll look into it and make the appropriate determination.

Cool Customer: You know, Mr. Grimm, I usually bill between $150 and $200 an hour for my time and there's no way I can break even on this transaction.

As the person addressed is on the payroll for considerably less, the superciliousness and hauteur are cut away and swept into the discard with a single motion, much like that of a hibachi chef. In addition, successful professionals who bill at these high hourly rates know how to deal with nonsense. Ever sensitive to possible jeopardy, the best way to avoid future problems is to settle the matter at once. Loose ends and dangling wires can become live and cause injury.

Putting a service person on his or her mettle—"Would it be possible . . . ?"—adds a little body English to your request, and appeals to honor—"In all fairness!"—have produced the desired responses even among the less than completely honorable. The earnestness and sincerity of "I need your help!" can also get you moving in the right direction.

Many of the people who can resolve your justified complaints are walking about with preconceived dispositions you can tap into with a few telling words. Look for early childhood beliefs, personal jeopardies and oft-repeated messages in the media for the raw material. With a little experimentation, you may be able to fashion a whole set of tiny rubber hammers with which to evoke the desired reflexes.

☐ Distinguishing Yourself

Onerous house rules imposed by sellers come in a myriad of shapes, styles and sizes but there are three general types. First, there is the inherently bad rule. I am not referring to the many outrages to which various minorities have been (and are) subjected, which lie beyond the scope of this work. The unequal treatment of women as buyers demonstrates that even a majority of the population may be discriminated against.

Women have been paying too much for too little too long. If, for example, a man buys a suit of clothing off the rack, minor alterations are routinely done by the seller and are usually included in the purchase price. However, if a woman buys a suit off the rack, it is usually wrapped at once *sans* alterations, unless the woman specifically requests the alterations be made, in which case she is routinely charged additionally. Unlike men, women are apparently expected to act as their own seamstresses and tailors or to pay somebody else to get the suit to fit. This inequality is under challenge and some major department-store chains have eliminated it.

Second, there is the reasonable rule unreasonably applied

(to you). You would ordinarily be willing to take a numbered ticket and wait your turn in a crowded bakery. However, if after waiting patiently the salesclerks were to call the numbers in random order as your number was about to be called, or certain favored customers who arrived after you were waited on without delay and without having to take a numbered ticket, you might well object.

Finally, there is the reasonable rule reasonably applied that adversely affects you disproportionately. You are at the airport. There is only one flight that can take you from A to B in time to keep an important commitment. There are twenty people already wait-listed. You'd like to get a preference that overrules the first-come, first-served policy, a reasonable enough formula that is being reasonably applied.

You can neutralize the negative effects of all three types of house rules. The most effective way to escape the adverse consequences of company policies and house rules is to distinguish yourself or your particular situation from the other cases covered by the generality. Demonstrate that you or the situation you are in is so different, the general proposition doesn't, or shouldn't, apply.

There are many ways to accomplish this. Your need is more urgent. You did everything you could to comply with the rule; your intentions were good. You are a source of large or continuing business, an old and good customer, or part of a group that does much business with the company regularly. Or, as a fallback in any case, the consequences of imposing the rule on you are especially severe. Almost anything will do if you can find a responsive person with authority.

Don't attack the company's policy. If you say the policy is ridiculous, you will encourage resistance and defensiveness. The other side will dig in its heels and you will be at an impasse. You will then have to play the game by the other side's rules or leave the field.

You can add some weight by stating your objective as a need. "I understand the policy but I *need* to get to Chicago this afternoon." Needs are clearly more urgent than mere preferences. The word fosters the suspension of disbelief among the genuinely service-oriented and gets the other side moving in the direction of satisfying the stated need.

Sometimes you may be able to use what Richard Bandler and John Grinder call "word salad" (syntactical sentences without any meaning) in their book on neurolinguistic programming, *Frogs into Princes.* "I have gone into places and spoken word salad and people have responded to me as if I had uttered perfect English. And of course you can embed crazy commands in word salad."

One of the authors wanted to buy some champagne for a party at his house. There were no stores nearby so he went to a restaurant and asked to buy a couple of bottles of champagne to take home. Told it was illegal, he replied, "Well, we're having a party and we come here a lot to eat and isn't there anything you can *do something!*" After a momentary pause, the other man responded. "Wait a second. I think I can do something." The man gave the bottles of champagne to himself, left the restaurant, handed the bottles over to the other man, and money in the form of a tip was paid.

Once you get the feeling that the world is an open system, that your options go beyond what is immediately apparent, you free your mind and spirit to look for other ways to loosen the seller's grip on rulemaking. On a trip to Boston I was scheduled to appear on a morning television program that originated in Needham. I approached a taxi parked outside the hotel.

"What's the flat rate to Needham?" (The flat rate is taxi

jargon for the prescribed, nonmetered rate.) The driver consulted his book.

"It's $28 each way, plus tolls."

"I'm going to be visiting a television station in Needham and will be there less than an hour. Then I'm coming back here. I'll give you $40 for the round trip and you're welcome to come in with me, watch the show and have all the doughnuts and coffee you want, on the house." The show always provides a table laden with these items.

He accepted without a beat. On the way back he told me he was delighted and that this was the best morning he'd ever had on the job. Note that whenever possible if you heighten or dramatize the specifics of your situation to remove yourself from the rule, the flat rate in this case, you will improve your chances. This was a round trip in a short time with free food and entertainment, not simply a taxi ride. You can finesse many arbitrary strictures, not by frontal assault, but by adroit cape work. Maybe those who've learned to do so smile more because they have more to smile about.

☐ Getting to Yes

You will be able to resolve many disputes with sellers to your satisfaction that otherwise would lead to deadlock if you make your objective "palatable." Unpalatable proposals are usually rejected outright. Even when they are accepted, they are often followed by a failure of performance. The other side may keep delaying delivery to you of what had been agreed, deliver less than had been agreed or renege entirely.

How can you increase this palatability quotient? Look for items of value to you that the seller can provide at little or no out-of-pocket cost to himself. It's always less expensive for the company to pay you with its own goods and services than to pay the equivalent retail value in cash. This is particularly true of many services the seller can provide by way of settlement with you. Some of these are essentially cost-free. It costs a hotel much less to give you a better room or a suite than it does to give you the difference in meals. The food obviously costs the hotel less than it charges but the room or suite costs it little or nothing out of pocket.

Unused capacity that cannot be stored is a highly palatable chip for the seller to proffer. If you find sufficient value in it to make you whole and happy, the dispute is easily resolved. Thus, in a situation described in detail in the next section, it was easy for an airline to give me bonus mileage toward an upgraded ticket or a free flight, the use of its VIP lounges and free headsets on coach flights. The value of all of this might have been perhaps $100 to me but the cost to the seller was approximately zero. It was an ideal solution for a minor disagreement.

Can you find or create other high-palatability items you'd like to have that would keep the real cost of settlement acceptably low for the other side? Look at the services routinely provided certain VIP customers, goods used in great quantity and a number of special frills and extras for which some customers are charged but which are larded on high-volume customers at no additional price. There is a natural tendency in the seller's mind to devalue stock items available in such abundant supply so that the hand practically plays itself if these items are acceptable to you. In fact, you may find the seller so willing to offer these lowest-cost items in settlement that you have to do a little gentle nudging to make a better deal for yourself.

I once appeared as a guest on a nationally syndicated television program. The show was paying me a fee and picking up the cost of the round-trip air fare to Los Angeles and one night at a hotel of its choice. Meals were not included, a not unusual arrangement for "B" guests.

When I arrived I asked the desk for a quiet room, as I was planning to leave on the first flight out in the morning. The room seemed acceptable, so I unpacked a few items, ordered a steak and some other food from room service and took a shower. About the time I finished eating, I got a call telling me a driver would pick me up in a few minutes and take me to the show. All went well.

However, later that night, as I was getting into bed, I

realized I'd been given a room under the hotel disco. A call to the desk was followed by a move to another room but this time somebody in the adjoining room was apparently a television junkie with a hearing loss. I wasn't exactly in the mood for sleep but I gave it a shot from another room on a different floor.

When I arose with the sun, I called the desk.

"Had a little problem with the room last night. I knew I'd be getting up at this hour so I asked for a quiet room when I checked in. The desk put me under the disco and I had to change rooms twice before I could get to sleep, at which point it was almost time to get up."

This person made the right sympathetic noises.

"As you know, the essential service you pay for when you rent a hotel room is the quiet enjoyment of your room. I certainly didn't get that last night."

More sympathy.

"Well, I'm not paying for the room . . ."

"Yes, sir."

"No, wait a moment. I'm not sure you understand. I'm not paying for the room because somebody else is paying for it but I think that in view of the inconvenience and the insensitivity you should 'comp' the other charges on the bill."

He agreed.

☐ The Paper Chase

If the other side is unmoved by your verbal attempts to resolve the matter in dispute, the next step is usually a letter. Here, less is more. Keep it to one page. Don't ramble. Don't criticize any of the company's employees and don't quote them. Quotations and criticisms usually create defensiveness and resistance. They tend to harden positions and they also mark your efforts as amateurish and therefore more easily ignored or settleable for less than would make you completely satisfied.

Keep in mind that anything you put in writing may be used against you. Don't admit any fault on your part as this may provide a convenient excuse for not giving you what you seek. Don't be dishonest but don't make damaging admissions against your own interests.

What's the motive most likely to persuade the other side to resolve this dispute to your satisfaction at this stage? After a good verbal presentation has failed, the most likely motivating lever is profit. Go with it. Present yourself as a profit opportunity.

You are the good customer of long standing who enjoys doing business with the other side. Your letter should be carefully composed, upbeat and amiable. Use expensive stationery. The difference in cost will be repaid many times over. First impressions do make a difference and they can be stage-managed.

You may sometimes prefer to create a special effect by going to the opposite extreme. Instead of high-quality stationery, the reverse, in exaggerated form, can also produce speedy relief. I've used an irregularly shaped piece torn from a (clean) brown paper bag, graced it with a handwritten scrawl and a few ink blots from a fountain pen (a fairly rare, and therefore memorable, sight in the ballpoint era). This visually unusual piece of correspondence, replete with grammatical errors, misspellings, deletions and interlineations, should look as though it had been composed by an anguished, unpredictable member of a subhuman species. When personally addressed to the chief executive officer or some other member of the company's top management, your letter tends to be rerouted rather quickly to an appropriate subordinate with instructions to handle the matter in a way that precludes any further correspondence. The net effect is to place you one step from a satisfactory resolution, especially if you were specific about what you wanted, and put a time limit on the other side for performance.

Another aspect of the paper chase involves a technique I call carboning the western world. You won't have to use this technique often. Most of the purchases you make will not require any remedial action. Preventive techniques, the selectivity principle and some degree of reasonableness on both sides will usually keep the transaction within acceptable limits. Of the relatively few transactions that do require further attention, one or a combination of the methods already suggested in these pages will neutralize most of them before it becomes necessary to write a letter. Of the remainder, only a small number will require carboning.

Here, your carefully framed complaint letter goes out to the other side accompanied by an impressive sheaf of copies, appropriately noted at the bottom of your original letter. With these carbons or photocopies you are seeking help from the addressees but, at least as important, you are putting the other side on notice that your call for help is reverberating and that the cavalry may be arriving soon with weapons drawn and at the ready.

You might consider sending copies to any and all of the following: your local, state and federal elected officials, the Federal Trade Commission, federal, state and local departments of consumer affairs, the state attorney general's office, the local newspaper(s), radio and television equivalents of the action reporter, licensing bodies and regulatory agencies, a trade association, the Better Business Bureau, executives in the various advertising media the seller uses and anybody else you think can help you. Be inclusive and err on the imaginative side.

A woman in Florida bought an organ, a big-ticket musical instrument, that failed to play satisfactorily from the day it was delivered. Despite the company's attempts to correct the problem, the organ continued to be a disappointment. After a while, the company stopped trying. Her unhappiness with the organ occasionally flared into outrage but she didn't know what to do. She was discouraged. Could I help?

I suggested that carboning the western world was worth a try. She did so and was delighted to report the receipt of a new organ that played perfectly in exchange for the defective one.

A woman in Pennsylvania bought a Japanese car that turned out to be a lemon and her anguished pleas fell on increasingly unhearing ears. She used the carboning technique and sent one of the copies of her complaint letter to (then) Prime Minister Tanaka of Japan (thus improving on my advice by also carboning part of the *eastern* world). The former Prime Minister, perhaps as a matter of national pride or out of gallantry, arranged for a new engine to be installed in the car by a local dealer.

Don't be disappointed if few of those carboned answer your letters. Most of the time you won't need a written response. The additional pressure created by the formidable list of people you've carboned is usually sufficient to move the other side to reopen discussions in a more conciliatory frame of mind, so that a satisfactory resolution is quickly reached.

☐ The Right Stuff

Sometimes the lock won't open easily. It sticks. It jams. It won't yield. You need something stronger than a key but less destructive than a hand grenade. You need the right stuff, a well-built record that gives you the required leverage. Building the record involves getting and keeping the documentation, the physical evidence and other hard, factual data you may need later in order to obtain complete buyer satisfaction. With a good record in your possession, the door opens easily and you walk in smiling.

In a Manila file folder or an envelope large enough to accommodate business letters without folding them, keep receipts, correspondence, warranties and brief, informal notes on conversations you've had with those on the other side with whom you've tried to reach an agreement. Include names, dates, times and who said and did what. A single large envelope or file folder will easily hold several year's worth of transactions in a way that makes for easy retrieval.

You should also keep Rolodex cards, alphabetically arranged by seller. Include the seller's name, address and telephone number (including toll-free and direct-dial numbers) and, as and when you develop the information, who reports to whom and whether to seek or avoid them. This will put at your fingertips an X-ray view of the company and indicate who among their personnel are the Scrooges and the Silas Marners and who the Lords and Ladies Bountiful, the good-natured, the fair-minded, the warmhearted and the open-handed. Good, easily accessible information about the other side is money in the bank.

In addition, keep your checkbooks, canceled checks and credit-card receipts for at least ten years and store them in a safe, accessible place.

One of the beneficial side effects of keeping such a record is that it makes you more sensitive to what material you may need and therefore more likely to take the necessary action to get and preserve it. Don't be shy about asking sellers to put their glib assurances and facile representations in writing. "You trust me and I trust you but what will we show the judge?" Said with a smile, to indicate you don't mean anything personal, this should be enough prodding to impel a legitimate businessperson who intends to keep his/her commitment to reduce it to writing. A written record is an aid to memory, encourages a better level of performance and can clinch a favorable outcome for you if the other side drops the ball.

As was suggested, getting the names of the people with whom you deal is a good idea but it doesn't assure accountability. Names can be slippery handles. The person who gives you his or her name may later deny ever having spoken with you or you may be given a false name. Names may also be withheld, especially if the anonymous malfeasant suspects your inquiry was not purely social.

Why not a handle of sterner stuff, a lever that can put something on the scoreboard for you fast? Say, for example, you've assumed the buying stance at a department-store counter but you're being ignored. The salesclerks continue to gossip idly among themselves, occasionally waiting on others out of turn. An alternative to charm or assertiveness might well be this little record builder.

Casually remove a small instant camera from your pocket or purse. Aim it deliberately, and presto, you've got an immediate likeness of the miscreant ignoring you. Your nonchalant pause at the counter for a moment should produce instant attention mixed with curiosity. There is a certain mystique about taking somebody's picture, particularly without permission. Aborigine tribesmen don't permit photographs of themselves in the belief that the photograph somehow gives the photographer control over them. Petty bureaucrats, subordinates, clerks, repair people, managers and other service personnel are even more chary about your owning their likenesses when they know they are in the wrong. You will almost invariably be asked for an explanation.

Clerk: What are you doing?

You: Oh, nothing.

Clerk: Did you take my picture?

You: (a bit shyly) Well, yes. That's right.

Clerk: What's the idea? Let me have that picture.

You: I was planning to show it to Mr./Ms. Big (the store manager, president, etc.) and explain why it's no fun to shop here anymore.

You should have no difficulty trading the photograph (reluctantly at first, and at the other's suggestion) for some super service reminiscent of the good old days. The other person is impelled to act, for the photograph is tangible. Your possession of it implies easy recourse, jeopardy, loose ends, controversy and continuation when the subject originally thought the matter could safely be ignored. The photograph is an unwelcome turnabout, a tangible reminder of vulnerability, of consequences, and action must be commenced at once to head off potential repercussions.

The technique has many other applications. Consider the effect on a restaurateur of a flashbulb photo of the mostly uneaten entrée of an overpriced, unsatisfactory meal. How might a television repair person react if, upon informing you the set would have to be taken into the shop and he could neither tell you when it would be ready nor how much it would cost, you simply focused your instant camera and coolly took his photograph? The effectiveness of the technique is roughly proportional to the reliability of the company management on the other side of the transaction.

There are lots of other "photographic opportunities." In a sidelight to a lengthy negotiation with a giant real estate company intent on getting the remaining tenants to relocate so that they could demolish our building and five others and erect a large cooperative apartment house, the lobby furniture was removed and massed in its place were scores of sinks and other plumbing fixtures taken from already vacated apartments. I tossed off a short note to the building and housing department suggesting this constituted harassment and enclosed an instant photograph of the newly "decorated" lobby. The lobby furniture reappeared shortly thereafter, apparently replaced by energetic elves in the wee hours while we were asleep.

A friend's son was involved in an automobile accident. Nobody was hurt but there was a great deal of property damage. His photographs of the site put him out of harm's way of legal liability and saved him and the family from protracted legal process.

Photographs are such convincing pieces of evidence (seeing is believing), they are often determinative in complaint situations. A few years ago, I received a parking ticket ($25) and had to retrieve the car from impoundment ($65). A single photograph showing there was no sign prohibiting parking where I'd left the car (as the ticket specified) got the ticket thrown out and all costs refunded.

On a short business trip to Los Angeles, my body clocks were still functioning on East Coast time when I left so I scheduled an early morning flight, checked out of the hotel, returned the rented car at LAX and entered the only airport eatery open for breakfast. I thought I'd order something light and easily digested that would sustain me until lunch en route. The menu listed "two eggs, any style." I ordered two three-minute eggs served in their shells and some dry rye toast.

"We don't have that."

I hadn't ordered eggs Benedict or sardou or a complicated omelet calculated to tax the chef. What could be simpler than a couple of boiled eggs? I'd arisen at about 6 A.M. All I wanted was a little nourishment, a lot of quiet and no hassle. Surely, this wasn't going to be a replay of the diner scene in *Five Easy Pieces.* How could it be? This was the Los Angeles International Airport, not that dreary diner. For a moment I considered taking the Hyatt Hotel limousine over to that hotel near the airport but it was too close to flight time. With an aircraft fueling at the gate, there was no place to go.

"Well, you have eggs, don't you?"

"Uh huh."

"And you also have a pot?"

"Yeah."

"And a stove."

"But we don't serve boiled eggs."

"Would you tell the manager I'd like to speak with him or her now?"

I unzipped one of the pockets of a carry-on bag and pulled out Mr. Instant Camera. As the manager approached the table, I took a close shot of the menu, focusing on "any style" eggs.

"We don't serve boiled eggs."

The negative answer preceded the question, always a bad sign.

"The menu does say 'any style' and I kept it simple. There's a strong truth-in-menu law here and I don't think either of us wants to test it. Let me have a couple of three-minute eggs in the shells and the photograph is yours. It's a management decision so it's up to you."

He got the picture.

☐ All in the Family

In the development of the public corporation, big business first divorced management from ownership. Millions of stockholders own the majority interests in the major corporations in this country but they are run by executives whose ownership, while sometimes large in dollar terms, represents only a small fraction of the whole. As corporations developed further, they began to create divisions and subsidiaries and to take over, merge and acquire other companies, resulting in a second major divorce, that of top corporate management from the actual day-to-day operation of the various parts of the corporation. This process has resulted in the appearance of gigantic corporations, the parts of which are often widely separated geographically and controlled by top managements hundreds, even thousands, of miles away.

Of the more than a hundred automobile manufacturers that used to make and sell cars in this country, only a handful now do so on any important scale and three dominate the market. Where there were thousands of independent hotels and motels in the Untied States, a few mammoth chains now control this market. Even a walk or a short drive to what used to be Pop Wilson's soda shop for an ice-cream cone may put you face to face with a subsidiary of a multibillion-dollar corporate behemoth.

An awareness of how these gigantic business organizations are controlled can add a silver-tipped arrow to your quiver at a time of need. You may, for example, occasionally want or need fast relief at the point of purchase but the local decision-makers, perhaps too emotionally involved in the matter or unaware of your skill and determination, steadfastly refuse to provide any. Lapses of this kind are not uncommon in hotels and department stores, where the managers and their assistants, rarely top corporate executives, are far from the watchful eye and direct supervision of a remote corporate headquarters and have begun to think of themselves as supreme authorities in their dealings with the customer.

Happily, it is precisely among these factotums and their deputies that instantaneous consciousness raising is most easily attained. When skillfully presented with the fact that higher authority not only exists and is readily accessible, but that management would vehemently disagree with both their bad decision and the way it has been imposed, these personnel shift quickly into "fast forward." Moreover, once the mistaken notion of omnipotence has been gently but firmly disabused, the newly humanized, former despot is usually in an especially generous frame of mind. Your original objective may therefore be raised without fear of overloading the circuitry.

If you are unable to obtain your accustomed buyer satisfaction, find out whether the seller is controlled by management located off the premises. Ask the switchboard or somebody else at the site whether this company has a corporate headquarters somewhere else and get the names of the president and chairperson, as well as the telephone number (including the toll-free number, if any) at headquarters. You may even discover some publicity material lying about that will give you this information.

You're now ready to move up the hierarchy locally. Don't be surprised if merely dropping the name of the lofty chief executive of the corporation into the conversation you're having with a service-oriented executive ends the dispute to your satisfaction. Initiate this discussion at least two levels above the point of the logjam at the site. This should disconnect any emotional involvement or investment the superior of the logjammer might have had in upholding his/her subordinate. After you've stated your case, you may wonder aloud whether the management at Conglomerate Industries, Inc., would be pleased with the way this matter was handled.

You can usually count on a great deal of insecurity among the executives in the subsidiary. Attrition and the operation of the Peter Principle have placed many such executives in jobs considerably over their heads. They're being paid more than they could earn elsewhere and they also have a fringe benefit stake in continuity on the job. They would like to avoid jeopardy while they tread water and advance toward retirement. Why make waves?

Occasionally, the magic won't work at the subsidiary and you have to call for help. Don't be disappointed if you can't reach top management at corporate headquarters. It isn't necessary. An assistant or executive secretary of a top corporate executive wields a great deal of clout at every level within the subsidiary companies. He or she can activate the proper executive at corporate headquarters as well as in the subsidiary and thus break your deadlock in a thrice.

Giant corporations spend large sums on public relations.

They are keenly aware of the value of their image. There is, therefore, no need, and certainly no advantage, to shrillness. Take the high road. No raised voices. Corporate headquarters is not the place for a venting of the spleen.

Understatement, implication and innuendo are the tools to be used here, not accusations, sordid details or recitations of who said and did what. A brief statement of the problem by way of general description is the best approach. Add details sparingly if asked for additional information. You are surprised, saddened or disappointed, as you and your family have had a long and pleasant relationship with the company and you hope somebody in management can help you. Maybe they're only having a bad day at Subsidiary Company, Inc. Might this person intercede or refer you to the best person to help you now?

If the call to corporate headquarters is long-distance, use the toll-free number or the subsidiary's local tie line. The subsidiary company's switchboard may sometimes balk at giving you this free access. If you say you're trying to avoid litigation and ask whether they'd be good enough to put you through to the main office, you should be accessed three out of four times.

If you are asked with whom you'd like to speak, the answer is the legal department. If the subsidiary's switchboard persists and wants to know *who* in the legal department, it's the general counsel or a staff attorney. After the call is put through, ask the person who answers for the name of the general counsel. The balky person who connected you via the local tie line may have remained on the line but, satisfied that you are actually calling the legal department, disconnects, and you are then free to have the person with whom you are speaking transfer your call to anybody you like through the main switchboard. If you've already been connected to the legal department, politely ask to be reconnected to the switchboard. When you reach somebody who sounds service-oriented, set out the facts briefly and ask what he or she would do for immediate relief if the situation were reversed. A few words coming from the top down are usually decisive.

☐ The Big Clock

If you've ever scrutinized the time sheets of a large law firm, no doubt you will have observed how these practitioners deftly slice a single hour into ten equal parts, like luncheon meat, and then neatly fold the slices into your bill, charging you for each one as if it were composed of the finest sturgeon roe or bunch of carats coaxed from the most ardently romanced stones. You are charged for the time it took for their elevators to arrive. You are charged for taxi-hailing time. You are charged while they wash their hands in the lavatory, all the while presumably thinking about your legal matter. However, should you arrive punctually, as is your wont, for a meeting at their office, you will be required to sit, waiting unproductively, while they slice up another hour to be added to somebody's bill at steep and mounting rates. This unilateral sensitivity about time is a common failing among sellers, a plague so far undocumented in the medical literature, for which a cure, however invasive, is long overdue.

The most useful approach I've discovered in dealing with these temporal outrages is a kind of principle that seems inarguable: if you don't get what you're paying for, you're overpaying. If you make a reservation for dinner at eight and have to wait until nine to get a table, you didn't get what you paid for (dinner at eight) and therefore you are, in effect, being overcharged. This idea may sound novel but it is gaining currency among the most respectable types. In fact, unless the restaurateur is a fool or a boor, he or she will send a drink or a bottle of wine to your table by way of apology.

When you use an air express service, time is obviously an important consideration and late delivery surely implies overpayment. In fact, one of the air express carriers has caught that notion nicely in its advertising: "It's on time or it's on us." However, *all* transactions take place within a time context and all sellers should be more sensitive to this aspect of the sale. Buyer satisfaction must include due respect for the customer's time. When it's not forthcoming, there are several ways to rectify the count.

Say, for example, you're buying a suit of clothes off the rack. The suit has been fitted by the tailor, chalked and pinned. You've signed for its purchase and you've changed back into your own clothing. If you then ask the salesperson about delivery, you will be given the standard delivery date (two weeks from Tuesday) or the salesperson may point to that date if it's posted on the wall, and you may even have to wait longer for actual delivery. If, however, you ask about delivery before displaying interest in any particular suit and before investing your time in selecting it, trying it on and having it fitted, the standard answer this time will probably be, "When do you need it?"

The timing advantage now lies with you, for in commercial dealings, you, the buyer, are in the strongest negotiating position before you've paid any money or signed a commitment to do so. If, before you commit to buy the suit, you are told it will take two weeks to alter but you know that nobody will be doing more than a half hour's work on it and you want to wear it on Friday, your response is simple.

"If I buy a suit or two now, I'm going to need to have at least one of them ready to wear before next Friday. I'm an easy fit. That's not a problem, is it?" The answer will probably be, "I'll take care of it for you." Wouldn't *you* accommodate the customer in similar circumstances?

There are several elements in this request. The word "if" makes the purchase conditional. You've committed nothing. "A suit or two" implies that you're a good prospect, somebody worth accommodating. The word "need" is excellent. Needs take precedence over mere preferences. "An easy fit" conjures the idea that only a little work will suffice, distinguishing your case from all others that involve people not so easy to fit, and gives the salesperson something to play back to the tailor, if necessary. "That's not a problem, is it?" puts the question in a positive way and practically answers it at the same time.

As a buyer, don't relinquish all control over time when sellers are so apt to take advantage. Who hasn't waited all day for a delivery or repair person who never arrived? Who hasn't listened to the wildly optimistic delivery date for the furniture given by the salesperson, only to wait and wait and wait, sometimes having even innocently thrown out the old furniture in anticipation of the delivery of the new, and then continued to wait dispiritedly in a practically bare house to which, out of embarrassment, nobody could be invited?

Time commitments are negotiable. Get a clear, unhedged commitment. "How soon will I have the washing machine delivered and installed?" If you're not satisfied, ask the seller to do better. "I need to have it by next Wednesday. That's not a problem, is it, Mr. Hadley?" Asked before you've made any commitment, it won't be. Then, get it in writing. Insist on a written commitment on the receipt. "Must be delivered on or before (month, day, year)." Have this signed or initialed by the seller. Not only will you get a more realistic idea of when you'll actually receive the goods, but it's also easier to convert an *obviously* fumbled ball (documented in the fumbler's own handwriting) to a concession than is a mere verbal misunderstanding between you and the salesperson. If sellers set the deadlines (which they do about four out of five times) to suit their own convenience and then fail to meet their own languid way of doing business, buyers are getting second-class treatment. Unless this sort of handling is accompanied by a discount, the buyer is overpaying.

Marketplaces also distinguish between prime and fringe time and an understanding of this concept can provide buyer satisfaction. All hours contain an equal amount of time but they are not equally valuable. Many sellers recognize this. For example, the parking garage adjoining New York's Metropolitan Museum of Art posted the following rates, effective September 1983: for cars entering between midnight and 5 P.M. two hours cost $6.14; however, cars entering between 5 P.M. and midnight, the rate was the same $6.14 until 10 A.M. The garage offered up to seventeen hours of fringe time for the same price it charged for two hours of prime time.

Many restaurants offer a restricted dinner menu between 5 and 7 P.M. at reduced prices. Movie theaters often feature reduced afternoon prices. As with second-day air delivery, lower-priority work should cost less. It should be possible to apply this concept to professional and other services. Why pay high-priority or preemptive-time rates for work to be done at the convenience of the seller?

The other side of this coin is to look for ways to get the most productive hours from sellers at their standard rates. People vary widely in productivity during the course of a typical day's work. The key split is between larks and owls.

Larks, those who rise and retire early, are extremely productive at breakfast and other early meetings, but tend to grow weary toward the close of the day. A cooperative meeting with a lark is therefore best scheduled early in the day. If I know that my lawyer (barber) is at his/her best in the morning and falters near the end of the day or, conversely, that he/she doesn't become fully awake until after lunch, I'll schedule my appointments accordingly. An adversarial meeting when your opponent has lost his/her edge can yield a competitive advantage.

All purchases are made in a time continuum. As a buyer you can take your share of the controls over this element into your own hands. Arrange to pay less for low-priority time and for failed time commitments, or get some other concession, and obtain peak performance at standard rates.

☐ Eliminate the Negative

As a buyer of goods and services, you are presented with printed contracts regularly and are routinely asked to sign them. There is the strong implication accompanying these proffered documents that you, the buyer, will affix your signature on the line indicated, and without delay. Should you hesitantly raise a thin-voiced query, you will be given to understand, sometimes even courteously, that the document is immutable. Your only alternative to accepting it in its entirety is to reject it altogether.

Of course, these contracts, drawn and approved by the seller's lawyers (and updated as statutory and case law dictate), heavily favor the seller and contain state-of-the-art pitfalls and traps for unwary buyers. So-called standard or form sales contracts, leases, securities brokerage account forms, hospital patient contracts and many other seemingly harmless documents routinely strip buyers, tenants, investors, patients and other innocents of fundamental property and personal rights.

Many long-disadvantaged segments of our population are learning to secure their rights. Women, children, old people, members of certain ethnic groups, the physically handicapped, the mentally ill and many others are at last gaining control over their lives. So can you. In other sections I will suggest specific ways to improve contracts with securities brokers, hospitals, insurance companies and other sellers. The principles involved have many additional applications.

In the case of life or automobile insurance, there are dozens of ways to reduce your premiums without any corresponding reduction of coverage, and the savings involve hundreds of dollars each year. A good insurance broker who isn't too aggressively sales oriented can provide valuable expertise, especially if you're prepared to ask questions and don't abdicate your own decision-making powers.

Beyond the losses inherent in paying too much and not getting full value, you may also be limiting your income because rules and regulations others impose on you without contest are drastically curtailing your opportunities for advancement. You can remove these restrictions and gain the freedom to improve your life without taking anything away from anybody else. An excellent example of such a limitation that is routinely imposed on millions of people but that has been finessed by some of the most successful men and women in the country involves the so-called company policy with respect to annual salary reviews.

The annual review serves to forestall employees' salary demands. The employee doesn't want to wait until the end of the year for a pay rise but employees who try to breach the company policy risk being considered pushy. The solution of choice for mobile employees (and those who'd like to be) involves self-nomination for a promotion or change of job title. Job changes may occur at any time of the year. The pay rises are usually more significant than the usual annual increments and you gain visibility and momentum as well. The policy is thus circumvented, not breached.

Self-nomination requires preparation and timing. The preparation is based on the principle that good news is always put in writing, while bad news is delivered orally. Avoid the use of the first person singular in communicating good news, as this may appear to be self-serving and opportunistic. It is always "we." This will be taken as modesty. You will appear to be a good team player, the kind of man or woman the organization needs and can count on, a good candidate for advancement.

The bad news is never committed to paper, where it can be duplicated and distributed with your name attached to it. It is presented in the first person plural, too, if you are involved, but verbally. If you've demonstrated commendable modesty in the taking of credit, the use of the first person plural in reporting the bad news will appear as a leadership quality, that of forthrightly taking your share of responsibility for the shortcomings of others. Your part in whatever produced the bad news will tend to be reduced to a minimum. The memorializing of the good news in memorandums using the first person plural will also permit you to report on good news you did not singlehandedly create, allowing for a little judicious usurpation. After all, you did say "we."

The timing factor in self-nomination is based on striking while the iron is hot, or at least heating. You are not constrained to wait for annual salary reviews as this policy does not apply to promotions or job-title changes. You may therefore choose the timing most advantageous to you. Look for opportunities to nominate yourself for a better job well before the end of the year. The focus of discussion should be on how this proposed change will better serve the company, not you, personally.

Request a meeting with a person who can effect (or at least strongly recommend) the promotion you have in mind. Put the request in writing, as paper concretizes it and also establishes a date for the request, making it harder to ignore. If ignored, a future request may refer to this earlier dated request with clinching specificity.

Take copies of your "good news" memos to this meeting. Arrange them in the order that will mean most to the person with whom you're meeting. Lead from strength. You don't have to discuss each memo but their visible presence adds substance to your presentation.

You've waited until you had some fairly important good news to report before requesting this meeting. You've demonstrated some of your abilities in your present job and would like the opportunity to contribute much more to the company. Some people in every organization are able to do more than others, to go beyond the mere descriptions of their job titles. Your capacity for greater responsibilities is a matter of record and you'd like to be considered for advancement.

Explain what you have in mind. The position need not currently exist. The important, larger moves are often made via job titles not previously on the company's table of organization but created for (and often by) the individual on the move.

If you're competent, asking will create a preference. Even if you don't get the position you had in mind, you should be able to attract a greater annual pay rise than would otherwise have been the case. If you think you've been inadequately recognized, nominate yourself again at an appropriate time. Every gain will compound in your favor. The people who succeed, in and out of corporate life, are those who continually extend themselves and go beyond their apparent "containers." Like seedlings that can grow even through concrete, all they need do is find nourishment, stay alive and follow their own nature.

☐ Help!

Have you ever watched small-claims court trials on television? Most of these cases involve plaintiffs who are suing their friends, neighbors and relatives. When was the last time you took your uncle to court? The cases I've seen in small-claims court are usually against businesses. Corporations are required to be represented by lawyers, so that the typical such case involves a plaintiff facing a lawyer for the insurance company representing the defendant corporation. The insurance company's lawyer may be defending a dozen cases each session and there are inevitable delays for one reason or another.

If you have a matter involving $50 or $75 or $200, you may have to appear in small claims court four or five or six times to have the case heard. There is a marked tendency for this court to compromise so that, even if you win, you may be awarded only fifty or sixty cents on the dollar. Significantly, you never see anybody collect a judgment on television, and the odds of doing so are only about even money, assuming you win.

There is a much better way to handle these disputes

against companies and professionals. You can get decisive help at no cost and without spending much time or energy. Once you learn to utilize the enormous resources of regulatory agencies, licensing bodies and departments of consumer affairs, you can obtain excellent, almost magical, results from your armchair, without even a single trip to the courthouse. My out-of-pocket cost per successfully resolved complaint averages less than a dollar via this route.

On one occasion, after the telephone company failed to correct some chronic problems on my lines, I requested help from the local public service commission office. A PSC investigator tested and monitored the lines, found precisely the problems complained of, but on some tortured reasoning completely upheld the telephone company. I was able to have all the jacks rewired as originally ordered and to exchange the faulty equipment. However, I also wanted a rebate for the poor service so I called the PSC in the state capital via a local tie line.

Aware that entry-level personnel would be unable to reverse the local PSC decision, I asked for the chief of the consumer section. The service had been extremely poor for a long time. The PSC investigation had confirmed troubles on my lines. I had been paying the full price for what should have been reasonably good service but had been receiving terrible service. Therefore, I had been paying for something not delivered and I wanted a rebate for this overpayment. Nothing by way of damages; only a rebate of some of my money. I asked the chief to intercede with the company on my behalf. The result was a $240 credit on our next bill.

Licensing bodies may also be used effectively in disputes with individuals as well as companies. It is almost invariably unnecessary even to file a complaint in these cases. Arrogant professionals and other transgressing sellers usually back off speedily in the face of an imminent grievance procedure before the duly constituted body with oversight jurisdiction. An accurate, specific reference to the proper ethics, grievance or disciplinary committee acts as a shepherd's crook in guiding these disputes toward speedy, entirely satisfactory resolutions.

Departments of consumer affairs (by whatever name they may be known locally) offer a variety of services. A good DCA is an invaluable resource. At no cost beyond normal taxpayer support, you, as a buyer, have a mechanism in place to help you prevent most common problems from arising, to provide free information, to supply professional mediation in resolving disputes, to enforce your rights as a buyer and to help you acquire additional rights through legislation. All of these services are immediately accessible to you from a local or state agency in most communities in the country.

A little skill in soliciting this help can make all the difference. Not everybody who answers your telephone call is the world's foremost authority on the particular problem you're trying to solve, however well intentioned they may be. Make it easy to get best results. Avoid the busy, early morning hours, Mondays and days after holidays. Call during the afternoon, well before the close of the business day, during the middle of the week.

Upgrade the quality of service. Ask for a supervisor or a specialist or a staff attorney without being offensive or patronizing. Focus on the problem you're having with the seller, not the problem you're having with the person trying to help you. Admit that the question you're asking is a difficult or technical one. Ask what this intake person would do to get expert help as soon as possible. If this person can't help you directly, don't be impatient. Let the person help you by suggesting an alternative. Try for a collaborative effort to help you, not a tug-of-war.

In any event, don't give up if your first call doesn't bring the magical remedy. It's easy to reach a higher level of expertise if you're not too intense. Intake people may be excellent at passing on your problem to a specialist but not so good at advising how to handle it. Be aware, also, that not all experts are equally effective, receptive or forthcoming. Keep asking. Find somebody who can help you or can direct you toward the help you seek. Almost every telephone room has a supervisor who is presumably better able to help you than those supervised. Use the same approach you'd employ if you were calling the switchboard of a large company. Be polite, courteous, tactful. "This is a complicated problem. May I speak with the supervisor, please?" Once you begin to move in the right direction, the hand practically plays itself. I've always received full cooperation from the New York City Department of Consumer Affairs.

After having my shirts done at a neighborhood laundry for several years, it came under new management and the service began to deteriorate. A shirt was damaged and management agreed to credit a certain amount against future work. Another shirt was ruined and one was lost. Attempts to reach a new agreement were delayed and then the laundry was replaced by a lamp store. Shirts could be picked up at another laundry but the latter denied any connection with the former.

It's a lot easier to deal with a business that's visible than with one that has ceased to operate and vanished, but I had an idea. If the laundry had been licensed by the DCA, it might have posted a bond. The bond would probably be backed by an insurance company and I could work this out with them.

In a call to the DCA, I learned that laundries are licensed in New York City and that this one's bond had been guaranteed by an insurance company in Keene, New Hampshire. I called the local office.

"I'm trying to avoid some litigation. Would you kindly put this call through to your legal department in the home office?"

In a few seconds I was explaining the situation to a staff attorney in Keene. The matter could be settled at once on the telephone, making it unnecessary for the company to be represented at a hearing before the N.Y.C. DCA. When the lawyer asked how much was involved, I told him without any hesitation: $93.10. He requested a letter from me for the file, with the assurance that the check would be cut on its receipt. It arrived within the week.

Once you get a little experience turning these situations about and realize that you can, if necessary, refer the matter to an outside agency for processing, it gives you the confidence you need to win the point with the seller in a single telephone call. To get a sense of what buyers were complaining about, I tape-recorded a number of conversations with commissioners of departments of consumer affairs, attorneys general and other complaints specialists and experts all over the country. I hired a typing service to transcribe some of the tapes.

High-level accuracy was not required. All I needed was to be able to read the material. The service quoted a per-page rate of $2.25. To eliminate the unexpected, we specified that a page contained about 25 lines and agreed on a delivery date. I said I had other tapes to be transcribed and looked forward to the delivery of the first job.

Delivery was late, accompanied by a bill for 176 pages of work at $2.25, a total of $396, about three times my estimate. The format of the typing was highly imaginative. Each line was indented to mid-page and the job was quadruple- and quintuple-spaced. Some pages had four and six words transcribed and the average page contained about 75 words. I called the manager of the typing service.

"Doesn't it seem ironic that the tapes you transcribed for me deal with consumer frauds and rip-offs and that's exactly why I'm calling you. Do you have a lawyer I can contact or would you prefer I call the attorney general?"

The manager said he'd refigure the bill. An hour of tape ran about 35 pages. Two 90-minute tapes should have run 105 pages. At $2.25 per page, the price was $236.25, not $396.

"We're getting there, but we're not there yet," I said. "There are only about 100 minutes of material on the tapes. The rest is blank; $2.25 times 35 equals $78.75 for one hour of transcribed material. Multiplying this figure by 1⅔ equals $131.25. Send me a corrected bill for $131.25 and I'll send you a check."

The manager asked whether the check could be picked up later in the day if he sent somebody with the corrected bill. I had the check ready.

Some case histories are more offbeat. Gary Walker of the New York City Department of Consumer Affairs told me this one about a consumer who asked the department to help arrange a credit to his account in the amount of $1,495. The man had bought an exotic parrot, represented by the seller to be "clean, safe and quiet" but it had proved to be, in the buyer's words, "noisy, dangerous and dirty."

The dissatisfied customer brought the bird back for a refund but the store's policy was that all sales were final. Home again with its unhappy owner, the unwanted bird bit the buyer's wife. It took three stitches to close the wound at the emergency room of a nearby hospital.

Another appeal to the store brought the same response. "All sales," the beleaguered parrot owner was told, "are final." Mercifully, the parrot was a slow learner, else it might have taunted its reluctant owners with grating repetitions of the store's policy.

An appeal to the N.Y.C. DCA resulted in the return of the unwanted bird for a full credit card setoff. The complaint experts were able to present the buyer's side of the matter a little more persuasively. The bird had been misrepresented as "clean, safe and quiet." This was clearly not the case. Rescission of the transaction was appropriate. The store, its feathers slightly ruffled, waived its "all sales final" policy and was reunited with the unwanted bird.

There's a joy and a power in self-help that I think is also salubrious. However, in the rare case when your own efforts don't put out a particular fire it's comforting to be able to call for help.

☐ For a Few Dollars More

The judicious spending of a surprisingly small number of dollars can provide a lot of buyer satisfaction. Given the low cost and the many benefits, it is as unproductive not to use this commercial solvent as it is to push a revolving door clockwise.

A lawyer and I arrived late to a business meeting. At the top of the ramp leading into the garage in the building in which the meeting was held, there was a large sign that read, "SORRY, WE'RE FULL." Nevertheless, the lawyer drove slowly down the ramp. A garage attendant ran up toward the car, waving his arms. "We're full up!" he shouted, but the lawyer continued to move forward at the same deliberate speed. He stopped the car, got out and handed the man two dollars. "We'll be here only about an hour," he said, and there was no further discussion. The other man handed the lawyer a stub without replying, and we headed for the elevators.

Say you are planning to have dinner with the boss or somebody else you'd like to impress favorably and you're going to be paying the check this time. You'll be going to an

85

expensive restaurant with the spouses or lovers. You'd like to be given red-carpet treatment.

If the restaurant is that delightful hideaway in the clouds, you'd prefer a window table. If not a window table, you want a choice location, not the table near the kitchen or other heavily trafficked area. If you begin with an excellent table, you are more likely to get better service. Those favored with the choicest tables are usually more demanding and freer-spending. The best waiters and captains are usually rewarded with the best stations. Thus, the benefits compound in your favor.

As this is a special occasion, you want to ensure excellence beyond the call for your party. Do some planning. Don't leave it to chance. First, make the reservation as far in advance as you can. This should give you an automatic preference as to seating arrangements, for few restaurants are fully booked far in advance. If you know a favored patron, mention it. Also, a reservation made in the third person carries additional weight. "I'm calling for Mrs. Brundage, at the suggestion of Jim Hill. May I ask with whom I'm speaking? I'd like a table for four next Friday at eight o'clock in Mrs. Brundage's name."

After the reservation is taken, point out that Mrs. Brundage is planning a special evening and that she would prefer her guests be given menus that don't show the prices, if this is possible. If the restaurant has such menus, you'll get them, of course. If not, you're one up on the restaurant because it couldn't accommodate this little nicety. Before the reservationist's feeling of being one down evaporates, mention the preference for a choice table.

"This is a rather special evening and Mrs. Brundage wants to be sure of a good *window* table, serviced by your best people. Which captain would you recommend? She'd like your help, Mr./Ms. ——— (play back the name you received earlier). Involve this person in the selection process and get the names of the maître d' and the captain recommended. "Are you sure they will be working next Friday evening?"

The more elements you leave unsettled, the surer you will be of random results and the greater chance there is for Murphy's Law to reign. Go to the restaurant when the named maître d' is working, about a day or two before this dinner is scheduled, and introduce yourself. Tell the maître d' when you will be dining at the restaurant. Explain that this is an important occasion and that you would appreciate this person's help in ensuring that it all goes smoothly.

Ask about the specials available that evening and whether dishes not on the menu are available. Ask whether the restaurant offers a *menu de gustation* that permits each diner to sample some of the restaurant's specialties. Give this person a small sum unobtrusively. Doing this in advance is an unusual move and you've put a few dollars in the hands of the very person who can help you, to thus support the seriousness of your purpose. This will be highly persuasive and you will be remembered. Why shouldn't you be catered to by name and treated as if this were your own palatial estate? It's all your for a few extra dollars and a little preparation. The boss (or other guests) will look at you with new respect, reflecting the way the restaurant staff greets you and waits on your every wish.

About twenty-five years ago, I observed the power of a single dollar bill. A friend and I visited some other friends at a resort hotel. We decided to stay for dinner. Before the meal the friend with whom I'd arrived, a man of few words, took the waiter aside. "My name is Al," he said. "Here's a dollar. If I like the meal, you get another one." The way Al was favored by that waiter made a lasting impression. He was treated like a visiting pasha while everybody else (including me) bleated himself hoarse, and waited.

Al hasn't forgotten either, apparently. At a recent dinner in a penthouse restaurant overlooking New York's Central Park, six of us were shown to a choice window table, courtesy of the maître d', who'd pocketed five dollars covertly proffered by Al.

An executive related this incident. The parking garage in which she usually left her car for the day was full when she arrived, so she drove to another garage a few blocks away. Much larger than the first garage, this one still had a number of vacant spaces and the rates were lower.

When she went to retrieve her car at the close of the business day, the place was a mob scene. Its one parking attendant was becoming increasingly overwhelmed by a rising tide of waiting customers whose tempers were visibly shortening. Late to a dinner party in a suburb of the city, wilting from the heat and the carbon monoxide, and aware that rush-hour traffic was building, she appealed in vain to the garage employee in the office. People continued to stream into the garage, some of whom were on a first-name basis with the overworked parking attendant. These latecomers were obviously receiving preferential treatment, while she and the others seethed. How might she have handled this frustrating situation?

I suggested that she might have gone to a public telephone on the premises and called the parking garage. When the office employee picked up her call, she would calmly have said the following:

"I need your help urgently and I'm prepared to pay for it." (Slight pause.) "I'm calling from inside the garage. I've been here for a long time and I don't feel well. I have stub number 14798 and I need to get out of here now. Please help me and

I will walk over and give you a five-dollar bill folded up so that nobody can see it. Stub number 14798. Thank you very much."

How could this approach have failed? She would have separated herself physically from the growing pack of others similarly situated, several of whom would have objected to her being given a preference while they waited. This separation would have finessed that problem for both the garage and herself. She was making a personal appeal: "I need your help . . . ." She didn't feel well. She was willing to pay for something to which she was entitled. She was asking, not demanding. The payment would be unobtrusive, thus avoiding the objections of others and possible embarrassment to the employee. Even if the office person were the one in twenty who would refuse this request, if the woman actually walked into the office and unobtrusively proffered a compactly folded five-dollar bill, her car would have been materialized promptly.

All sorts of services that can make life easier and more pleasant are abundantly available at surprisingly low cost. My wife and I spent a few days at a hotel in Key Biscayne a few years ago. At a buffet brunch, a horde descended on the food, seemingly oblivious of everything inedible. I noticed a slightly infirm, elderly couple obviously overwhelmed by the crush. Their efforts to get close to the buffet tables were stymied and they were being engulfed. I stopped a passing busboy.

"I'd like you to do me a personal favor," I said, handing him three dollars. "See those two people over there? They can't handle this mob. Seat them at a table and get them whatever they want to eat." He was happy to oblige, and a short time later, the elderly couple were enjoying their meal.

There are so many times extremely small amounts of money can make a big difference. Say your young child is going to take a long train trip alone. Upon seeing your child off at the station, ask the crew member directing the flow of boarding traffic who is the best person to keep an eye on the child. Take that person aside and give him or her five dollars. Explain that you need a little help in watching over the child. Get his/her name and then introduce your child. Tell your son or daughter that Mr./Ms. So-and-So is the person to ask for if your child needs any help.

Service people are aware of the power of a few extra dollars and, if approached with sensitivity, will almost invariably provide value way beyond the trivial sums involved. Service people are people. Others may have treated them with less than the full accord and dignity they deserve. You must avoid this approach. Your request is *not* a demand. You are asking for help. It's a personal request, best done quietly and unobtrusively. "I need your help. . . . Would it be possible for you to do me an important favor?" You're not paying for the service. The money is not a symbol of your largesse, not a tip or a gift, and it's best not made much of, but simply handed over, and perhaps in an envelope.

In addition to the situations in which you are handing over money for the purpose of obtaining a particular special service, there are several people who provide little services for you on a sporadic basis throughout the year or who *would* do so, or *might* be disposed to doing so, if you acknowledged them with an annual or seasonal small gift or gratuity. We're not talking about commercial bribery here or any major expense. Such things as Christmas gifts are a fact of business life. You may be certain that your competitors are giving them; not to do so might put you one down and that's surely not recommended.

Mere verbal outpourings of appreciation to an important (to you) executive secretary, your doctor's receptionist, who understands the value of your time, helps you avoid long waits in the doctor's waiting room and who remembers to call you if the doctor is running late, however heartfelt or effusive, are all right, to a point, but they are constituted, after all, of the finest gossamer no matter how well crafted and personalized. Expressions that embody the concrete of gifts and gratuities (albeit not large ones) generally carry greater weight and they don't preclude verbal accompaniment, however lyrical.

Some tacticians of largesse have suggested that annual gifts be dispensed at Thanksgiving instead of Christmas. Your thoughtfulness stands out and is not part of the blur of Christmas giving. You don't mix what many celebrate as a religious holiday with commercialism, and Thanksgiving also arrives earlier, putting you a full month ahead of your competition in building goodwill. In any case, it's a salutary idea to share your good fortune with others and to express your thanks with a small gift or gratuity to those who may have helped you in some way. Zoroaster summed it up rather neatly: "When thou eatest, give to the dogs, should they even bite thee." Casting bread upon the waters has a long tradition.

☐ Reasonableness

In the Hollywood movie version of the life of Rudolph Valentino, there is a scene in which a wealthy dowager is on the dance floor with (then) gigolo Valentino. The woman, obviously pleased, leans toward Valentino and says, "Will you be free next Tuesday, Rudy?" Smiling disarmingly, Valentino replies, "I may not be free but I promise to be reasonable."

A worthy sentiment, to be sure, and one that underlies the approach proposed in this section. If you recall, the first principle I discussed involved the concept of selectivity, the idea that many wrongs would not be pursued. You would take up the cudgels only when you were clearly in the right and would factor in a consideration of the size and scale of the transaction, choosing not to become embroiled in trivial disputes. The same sense of propriety that governs the selectivity principle also guides the attitude of reasonableness.

It is important to maintain a proper balance with the environment, the system and the marketplace. Conflict and controversy should not play a major role. If your docket is crowded, take it as a sign that your balancing mechanism should be checked. You may need to lighten up. Even the poor players on the other side who may be abusing you or their position or the resources of the system are people, too, and as such have their entitlements.

In obtaining relief, minimal force levels are recommended and your responses should be graded. Avoid overkill. It is unnecessary and unseemly to damage others and this should never be your objective. You will encourage the other side to keep their commitments and you will keep yours.

The methods and techniques suggested in these pages have all been kitchen-tested by me and others. They have a long track record of winning at every distance from sprints to marathons. They work because, no matter how complex, people cannot escape their humanity. If you follow them, you will develop a surprising amount of assurance and power.

You can cause effects. You need no longer be at the mercy of circumstances beyond your control. The wisest man I know once said that good circumstances and bad circumstances are only circumstances. They are not the final determination. If you have sufficient will and spirit, the game remains in progress until you like the final score. This understanding gives you enormous strength and resilience. The responsibility for using this power should not be taken lightly.

There are many ways to abuse power. None is acceptable. In applying the strategies herein, you are essentially defending yourself against certain kinds of nonsense all too abundantly found when money is involved, as it always is in the various marketplaces. It is entirely possible to abuse power by defending yourself so vigorously that you become the aggressor.

As you must guard against mounting a personal attack on some petty wrongdoer, you should also never take advantage of another person's honest mistake. If, for example, the seller adds a bill of sale incorrectly to his/her own disadvantage, an aware buyer is obliged to point out the error. If you are given too much change it would be unconscionable to keep it, knowingly.

These obligations must be taken seriously, and not simply because they represent the right ways to act. The insignificant give-backs are as nothing compared with the blunting and coarsening of the instrument these petty misappropriations create. If you are finely honed and in the right, you are virtually invincible, provided you don't quit on yourself if some miscreant throws you for an occasional loss. When you win big, you may not even remember the little setbacks you encountered along the way. It isn't the winners who have to stay late watching the films of last week's game, with its mistakes and lost opportunities, or even worse, have to keep replaying the bad tapes in their own minds. If you stay well honed, you will develop a power of conviction that can drive right through walls. On the other hand, if you lose your moral compass and corrode your own sense of right and wrong with unethical expedients, this fine edge is destroyed and your power wanes.

This book is intended to be useful to buyers but the seller must be treated fairly. If we are to demand full value for our money from sellers, we have a corresponding obligation to stop free riding on the seller's vehicle. Some people buy an expensive dress for the purpose of wearing it to an important social or business function, intending to return it with some false explanation for a full refund after it has served its purpose. A man I know brags of obtaining illegal discounts on certain services with a bogus identification card. Somebody else uses an electronic bluebox to defraud the telephone company.

These people, and thousands of others, rationalize such

acts on the basis that they are only evening the score for a number of wrongs dealt out to them in the past or that the company from which they are stealing is large and impersonal and the loss inflicted trivial and unimportant. These and myriad other petty crimes have no place whatever in the method recommended here. They unduly burden the system and impose a price we all must pay. These polluters of the community bloodstream leave the cleaning up to others.

Those who succumb to these antisocial practices also pay a heavy price. They quietly undermine their own character, causing them to lean ever harder on the marked deck, the phony credential, the big fix and the rigged bid, making them increasingly unfit to compete in the universe on an equal basis. All social and business relationships, like games, have rules. Bluffing, for example, is an integral part of the game of poker but cheating is totally unacceptable. All is *not* fair in marketplaces regardless of your role.

There are practical reasons for acting properly. One is that right action adds conviction to everything you say and do. Others react to this force, this authenticity, and resolutions to disputes are often found quickly and efficiently that might otherwise have resulted in impasse. The Zen monk Unmon put it well: "When you walk, just walk. If you sit, just sit; but whatever you do, don't wobble."

There are many people from whom you wouldn't buy a used car. Study them without becoming involved with them. Learn what it is about them that makes them inauthentic. Are they not dissynchronous? Is not their behavior at odds with their statements? They don't keep commitments when it's inconvenient. You can't count on them so you *dis*count them.

The choice is clear. Behave badly and dismantle your on-board internal guidance systems, impair your own senses, and get increasingly less reliable results, or behave well, build your character into forceful solidity, become more efficient and effective and move in any direction you wish, confidently, with ease and comfort and without burdening the system. I emphasize this approach not only because it is right but also because it is practical. I do so not as Pollyanna but as the person recognized by *The Guinness Book of World Records* as the world's most successful complainer.

As you develop your skills in resolving these disputes, you may be surprised to find how easily things in the marketplace begin to fall into place for you. The real champions make the tough plays look easy by managing to be in the right place at the right time with the right stuff. The artist conceals his or her art. So, too, the accomplished complainer prevents or avoids most of the potential pitfalls and confrontations.

Avoidance and prevention are not dramatic but they're extremely effective in making life smoother and more pleasant. If you can see the latent ambiguity in the other side's promise or the deal seems too good to be true, clarify it. Don't sit back and wait for something to go wrong so you can wipe out the bad guys. A reasonable person doesn't seek ways to add notches to his or her gun belt. Avoid collisions and confrontations. Keep a sharp lookout so that you have ample time to take evasive action if necessary.

There are many legitimate ways to win. You can come from behind with two out in the ninth or drive down the stretch between horses to win by a nose at the wire in a tight photo. There's much less wear and tear involved if you can coast home in front wire to wire. When the great American miler Glenn Cunningham was asked how he won races, his answer was simple: "I get in the lead and stay there."

This confident, easy, loose feeling of the front-runner puts a lot less strain on you, and you, in turn, are less likely to transfer pressure to the system. This is the method of choice recommended here. It's cleaner and much more forthright than sitting back, waiting for something to go wrong that you should have prevented and then beating the daylights out of some poor misguided fool who tried to take advantage of you.

As you will not entrap or lure others into overplaying the hand so that you may extract a penalty, you will also be reasonable in your demands in a proper case for legitimate complaint. Don't try to force a particular malefactor to recompense you for every past wrong you ever suffered. I once had the pleasure of meeting the man who wrote the original made-for-television movie that launched the *Kung Fu* series. I reminded him of a line I remembered fondly from the script that embodies this doctrine of reasonableness. At a distance of about fifteen years, I hope the following is accurate:

Avoid rather than hurt,
Hurt rather than maim,
Maim rather than Kill,
For all life is precious
Nor can any be replaced.

PART TWO

How to Deal with the Worst Offenders

□

A relatively small number of the items you buy are extremely high-priced. A bad purchase of one of these big-ticket items may be expensive and the unhappy consequences in such a case almost invariably involve more than money. Thus, these few sellers can cause a great deal of damage—and they do so all too often. Files of federal, state and local agencies bulge with precisely such complaints, and court records of the heavy losses inflicted on innocent buyers by these worst offenders grow increasingly voluminous daily. Unfortunately, these sellers are usually glib, often professional, and almost always favorably situated, by virtue of fine print and fancy footwork, to escape redress.

My objectives, as set forth in Part Two of Satisfaction Guaranteed, *are twofold: prevention and cure. The primary emphasis in these high-risk situations is to provide complete buyer satisfaction by avoiding any and all untoward fallout. If, however, this objective cannot be met on a rare occasion, the emphasis shifts to obtaining another kind of satisfaction: namely, the speedy receipt of a compensatory sum sufficient to pay in full for all of the pain and loss.*

□

☐ Lawyers

You have many safeguards when you deal with medical practitioners. As a late-model human, you have the benefit of advanced design. Many homeostatic mechanisms are quietly working in concert to bring you toward the norm, should you fall ill, despite incompetent or neglectful medical care. You can also monitor the situation fairly easily. You know whether you feel better or worse after following your doctor's advice and, in the latter event, can seek more effective care before it's too late. You have also learned to seek "second opinions" before following radical medical or surgical advice.

None of these important safeguards protects you from semicompetent legal practitioners. Legal problems usually get worse, not better, if neglected or handled improperly. You also have no easy way to determine that your legal matter is receiving poor treatment until it's too late. If your lawyer prescribes the wrong legal "medicine" or sits on his hands, even if you are astute enough to realize it before a final adverse determination, your legal position is likely to be

101

undercut, irreversibly damaged and perhaps rendered worthless.

Finally, most other lawyers will not give you "second opinions" while you are "represented" by somebody else. They may be willing to discuss your firing the first lawyer and hiring them but the ethics of the profession (which, you may be sure, the first lawyer will remind any other prospective lawyer) protect the semicompetent lawyer from being second-guessed by a competent one until the former is fired. You may substitute attorneys only to find that many of the defects already woven into the fabric of your legal matter by the first practitioner are permanent, even decisive, weaknesses. More than likely, the first lawyer also expects to be paid or has already been paid for his shoddy, negligent and damaging work, piling wasted money on top of wasted time and detrimental work product.

Difficult as it is for you to distinguish an excellent lawyer from a semicompetent one, especially early on, before you've hired the latter, it's important to be able to do so as the stakes can be extremely high. A great sum of money, your personal happiness (and that of those closest to you), even your life, may hang in the balance.

Suppose, for example, through no fault of your own, you were involved in a serious automobile accident. You would not ordinarily be in a good position to estimate the severity of your injuries and might not discover their full extent for years. Broken bones are fairly obvious but what about organic brain damage that results in permanent, but only partial, impairment? What about other permanent injuries like those that restrict blood flow and will produce serious nerve damage over the course of time? How would you know that you've sustained a number of other physical injuries that will become progressively worse? Most victims of serious accidents go through an initial phase of "denial" in which they do not admit, even to themselves, that they have been seriously and permanently injured.

The lawyer who handles this case will often be the decisive factor in whether you ultimately accept $25,000 or several hundred thousand dollars and the same practitioner may also make the pivotal difference in the future state of your health. If you go to an ordinary, semicompetent "negligence" lawyer (negligent lawyer is all too often closer to the mark) and are unfortunate enough to hire him or her, this lawyer will indelibly chart the future course of your litigation. Without knowing it, you will be on your way into the drainage the moment you sign the retainer agreement.

Here's the way the strong currents in the drainage tidal waters typically work against you. First, even if you think you've been severely injured, you are in no position to evaluate the injuries in monetary terms in a negligence lawsuit. Therefore, you don't know you can get one of the best litigators in town to take your case. The semicompetent practitioner listening to your account of the accident across the desk won't admit he/she is not able to judge the value of your case and will certainly not suggest you would do better to retain somebody else as soon as possible.

What is immediately apparent is that the case is worth a sizable (but undetermined) amount to the lawyer if he/she can at least get you to sign a retainer agreement. Any lawyer can serve a summons and complaint on the other side (even if some of the possible defendants are not included) but few can prepare and try the case with distinction. However, the semicompetent lawyer knows that most cases are settled prior to trial (especially if plaintiffs accept only a fraction of their value). The semicompetent gets your signature, inadequately prepares your case (destroying much of its value forever), underestimates your potential recovery, exaggerates the risks of trial and, by degrees, convinces you to settle what might have been a $500,000 case for $40,000. The lawyer typically gets about one third, a darned good payday for some routine paperwork. The client gets mauled.

It's extremely important to understand how inadequate preparation, with which poor results are highly correlated, works against you so that you may hire armed guards, if necessary, to prevent it from ever entering your life. Medical evidence, most valuable when collected early, will be neglected until later. The semicompetent lawyer may know some cooperating doctors but they will not, in most cases, be first-rate specialists in the kinds of injuries you sustained. The investigation will be inadequate or nonexistent. Investigators cost money, and the semicompetent (who doesn't yet, and may never, know your case is potentially of great value) won't be as willing as the real pro to spend money on this important aspect of the case. Invaluable photographic evidence will not be produced by your side. Witnesses that might have been of great help to your side will not be interviewed early on (before the other side has had a chance to reach them and begin to color their recollections), if at all.

The semicompetent will also be overmatched by the legal talent defending, practically ensuring a trial or a low settlement. Had you hired an excellent lawyer (known in the profession for winning big jury verdicts), the other side would have been encouraged to settle at a fairly lofty number long before the trial date, at which they'd be risking much more. Against a semicompetent, there is no incentive to offer a large settlement and certainly no need for haste. That money will be earning interest for the insurance company, instead of you, for years.

The other side's lawyers, usually house counsel of the defending insurance company or experienced outside counsel, will not be idle. They are being paid for their work so it is in their interest to do the work. They will interview witnesses. They will send out experienced investigators to get the evidence. They will certainly not offer to share evidence damaging to their side with your lawyer, nor is this their obligation. Thus, the photographs of the automobile in which your face was sculpted into the windshield by the force of the impact (and which could not have failed to impress a jury) will never be taken but the photographs showing no damage to the engine block (totally irrelevant to the case) will be produced for your lawyer if photographs the other side has are belatedly demanded. The difference between hiring an excellent lawyer to handle this case and hiring an ordinary one or a barely competent or an incompetent one may thus spell the difference between a life of poverty and misery for the victim and his family and a decent life with some dignity for the victim and his family and his heirs.

The widespread and wide-ranging dissatisfactions and frustrations clients generally experience in dealings with their lawyers have been recorded over the centuries by a large number of the most distinguished authors in the English language. Their testimony cannot be ignored and should not be taken lightly. It is inarguably extremely difficult to get what you have every right to expect when you buy legal services. In this chapter my objective is to offer some useful guidelines for greatly improving your chances for buyer satisfaction. The questions addressed are: do you need a lawyer and, if so, how can you hire the right lawyer at the right price, keep the lawyer-client relationship good and help move your legal matter to a satisfactory and timely conclusion. Given the many pitfalls and almost complete lack of effective discipline in this important sector of the marketplace, it will be difficult to answer these questions usefully, especially in the limited space available. Difficult, admittedly, but maybe not impossible.

Do you need a lawyer? As you don't rush to a doctor's office with every nick or scrape, so, too, you don't need to pay a lawyer every time you think you need "legal" services. You may not need to pay anybody at all, and even if you do, it might not be a lawyer. As lawyers are the most difficult professionals to work with satisfactorily, if somebody else can answer your need, you're way ahead of the game even if you have to pay him/her. Your real need may be for information and an amazing amount of it is available free. Books, kits and manuals abound. If these readily available materials are not sufficiently helpful, a good librarian can suggest other free or inexpensive sources of information and point you in the right direction to secure them.

There are also hundreds of federal, state and local departments, agencies and bureaus. These are often conveniently grouped and listed in the back pages of telephone directories. These governmental appendages are bulging with lawyers, some of whom are genuine experts in their respective specialties. Once you get by the initial screener of the calls, you can obtain a great deal of reliable, free information from a legal specialist in a single call.

Say, for example, you have a complicated, highly technical question about insurance law. You'd like a specific answer and the section and subsection of the law that governs the matter. If you call the state department of insurance (often a local number or a local number with a tie line to an out-of-town office) and can reach the chief counsel's office or that of a smart staff attorney, this person or somebody to whom your call will be transferred can give you the answer in about four minutes at the cost of a quarter. You may even ask to have a photocopy of the relevant section of the law mailed to you. Compare this for accuracy, speed and cost with the average lawyer's performance.

Your elected state, federal and local representatives also

maintain offices that employ many lawyers who are available to your calls for free advice and service. On other occasions you may want to use a law library but are intimidated by its size and complexity or don't think you can gain access to one. The most complete law libraries, and the easiest ones for the general public to use, are research law libraries.

To obtain access to a research law library, call a local law school and ask the librarian whether you may arrange to use the library. If you are a graduate of the undergraduate school, say so. If you can accomplish your purpose in a single morning, afternoon or evening, say so. Unless you pick a time near the ends of semesters, when these libraries are being used to capacity, if you're fairly courteous, you should be able to use a law school library for a limited period of time (a couple of weeks or so), especially if you state your willingness (should you be turned down) to use only a small amount of fringe time. These libraries stay open late at night and on weekends and many holidays. Many law school libraries are federal depository libraries; that is, they receive a free copy of all U.S. Government publications and they are obliged to make these publications available to the public.

If a law school library is unavailable or inconvenient, you may want to use a working law library. The county courthouse librarian may permit you access to its library and many lawyers (perhaps even somebody in the legal department of the company that employs you) can arrange to have you admitted to a private law library. In addition, a public librarian in almost any sizable community may also be able to direct you to a law library you may use on a temporary basis.

There are times, to be sure, when you will need a lawyer. If, for example, you're dealing with somebody (anybody) who is represented by a lawyer, you should also be represented and not by the same lawyer, no matter how friendly you are with the other principal. If you are a defendant in a litigation, are under an investigation by an agency of government, accused of a crime or are involved in any of a large number of other situations in which legal formalities have a role and where you don't get a cost-free opportunity to correct your errors and omissions, by all means hire a lawyer. In short, whenever the potential upside or downside is important to you, you may need to consult a lawyer.

As most lawyers are better able to prevent disasters and other untoward consequences before they happen than to cope with them effectively afterward, the time to hire the lawyer is sooner, not later. See your lawyer before you sign the contract, for example, when it's relatively easy, in the sanguinary flush of anticipated profit to the other signatory, to make a few changes in the document and it is extremely inexpensive to do so as well. Don't wait to see your lawyer until somebody is suing you on the contract. By then the deal, and possibly the relationship you had with the other party to the contract, has gone sour. The problem is then real, not imaginary, the kind most lawyers are less well equipped to handle and the kind that costs much more money to extinguish, win or lose.

If you're at least moderately successful and lead a fairly active life, no single legal practitioner (or even a single law firm) will be able to handle all of your legal affairs if satisfaction and price are of any concern to you. The key to your success with lawyers lies in selecting the right one for the particular job of work to be done. The right lawyer for you isn't necessarily the best lawyer in town or the most expensive one. Many kinds of legal work, including some of the most frequently sought legal services, demand little of a lawyer and overkill in these cases is needlessly costly.

In 1975 the United States Supreme Court decided that it was unconstitutional for a bar association to ban advertising by lawyers. Since that decision, so-called legal clinics have widely advertised their prices for a number of fairly routine legal services. It is precisely these kinds of advertised services by legal clinics that do not require super (or superexpensive) legal talent. In fact, many of these services do not require *any* legal talent at all. They are more clerical in nature than legal. The uncontested adoption of a child by the spouse of a natural parent, for example, is not more complicated than filling out four easily understood pieces of paper and meeting with a judge for ten minutes or less. Unless the child tells the judge he/she is a kidnap victim, there is little that can go wrong. In fact, a clerk of the court will go over the four pieces of paper and help you correct any errors you may have made. The only reason you need a lawyer in cases like this is that the law (usually written by lawyers) demands it. Legal clinics can offer such services inexpensively because they are uncomplicated, nonadversarial and not labor intensive or time consuming. With a little intelligent use of available office technology, these services are easily and quickly dispensed.

Legal clinic advertising emphasizes price. An initial consultation might cost between nothing at all to perhaps $25. An uncontested divorce, a routine incorporation or an uncomplicated adoption is available for about $250 or less, almost anywhere in the country. A little comparison shopping will quickly locate the best price in your area for the routine service offered. One of the by-products of this advertising is that, now that clinic prices are common knowledge, nonclinic legal practitioners are a little more tractable in their pricing of similar services.

Legal clinics are a good choice for a few routine jobs but what if you need a legal specialist and excellence will make a great deal of difference to the outcome? Here's where the selection process often becomes a maze from which few clients emerge with their dignity, their rights and their wallets intact. Lawyers are available in a bewildering welter of shapes, sizes and varieties and there is no shortage of them. There are more than 600,000 lawyers in this country, one for every four hundred men, women and children. There are more than 150 specialties in law (more than in medicine) and all of these services are available over an astonishing range of competence, effectiveness and price. How can a buyer make an intelligent choice?

There are several referral services, a number of legal directories and a much greater number of friends, relatives, fee splitters and other interested and disinterested parties who will volunteer the names of their version of precisely the superstar lawyer you need to produce the result you want at a price you can afford, or perhaps a bit more, "but it's worth it." Referral services and directories have biases built into their compilations that you don't know and therefore cannot begin to decipher, and volunteers, especially those not conspicuously successful, are usually best avoided when you're engaged in serious business. If you consider yourself a lucky person, these methods should yield no better than random results; if not, you are probably hiring an accident waiting to happen to you at the wrong time and place.

Before you proceed, consider whether you should hire a lawyer who is part of a firm or a solo practitioner. You can get good and bad results either way but I recommend the former. First, nobody known by his peers to be incompetent is likely to be sought out or accepted as a member or associate of a law firm (especially a good one) so you automatically finesse many problems. Of course, the Three Stooges may occasionally open an office but they aren't likely to have much of a track record over the long run.

Members and associates of law firms also freely consult with one another, to your advantage. The firm or partnership can also more easily afford to hire legals and paralegals, often on a pooled basis. Some of the routine work on your matter may be assigned to these people by your lawyer at much lower billing rates to you. The solo practitioner would presumably be charging you his/her own higher rates for this routine part of the work. A firm or partnership is also more likely to use up-to-date and efficient office technology, which translates into time and money saved for you.

A single practitioner, on the other hand, does not so freely get advice from colleagues in close proximity and is more limited to his/her own knowledge and skills. The single practitioner has nobody with whom to share the legal work to be done and thus his/her time is preemptive, for the most part. If he/she is doing task A for client X, your work sits unattended. There is only so much that can be done at a time and delays tend to be endless. As there is nobody on the site to whom your matter may be assigned, after it loses its natural momentum, it tends to become stale.

There are also some commendable checks and balances built into the firm or partnership that are absent when your lawyer is a solo practitioner. The other lawyers are, in effect, looking over your lawyer's shoulder. Without this kind of supervision, the solo practitioner may be tempted to go overboard in his/her handling of you or the work to be done. Idiosyncratic behavior and other personal crotchets, often most unwelcome in somebody handling an important legal matter for you, are more likely with the solo practitioner.

What's the next step in the selection process? I've gotten referrals to excellent lawyers by calling the best law school in my community and asking the professor who heads the department in which my matter lies to suggest a good law firm and lawyer within the firm. A current law school catalog will give you the names of these department heads or you may call the dean's office of the law school. Don't be reticent.

Most professors are professorial and enjoy giving advice, especially when it's sought.

"My name is Jane Rivers. Who is the chairperson of the trusts and estates department, please?"

The next call is to his/her office. To make it easier, you may also ask the dean's office when this person has regular office hours and call during these hours.

"This is Jane Rivers, Professor Hanna. I wonder whether you would be kind enough to suggest the names of a couple of very good lawyers who might be able to help me with a complex trusts and estates matter."

If you get only one name, thank the professor and ask whether he/she can suggest another lawyer, "so that if there's a conflict I don't have to bother you again."

Another way of developing a short list of good names of prospective lawyers for your purpose is to ask successful and practical business and professional people for recommendations. People who are both practical and successful don't like to waste time or money and they expect good results. Their recommendations should reflect this. However, you must take into account the possibility that your legal matter and theirs may be different enough so that their good result may not necessarily imply the same for you. If you decide to hire a lawyer recommended by a friend you are, of course, not bound by the fee arrangement he/she had with the lawyer. You are free to negotiate a better deal.

The third method for selecting a satisfactory legal specialist is to pick a lawyer who has been a chairperson (or even an active member) of a bar committee in the particular specialty you seek, or a speaker or teacher of other practicing lawyers in the same specialty. These commendable activities should not occupy a large part of your prospective lawyer's time. You are compiling a short list of skillful and effective *lawyers,* not recruiting budding politicians, teachers or scholars.

Good legal directories will supply some of this information (as well as other biographical data) and the rest is available from your local bar association. Legal directories will also tell you whether or not a lawyer is a member or associate of a firm. The most widely used is Martindale-Hubbell, a seven-volume compilation available in many general, and virtually every, law library, and in the offices of thousands of lawyers. A good law library would be likely to have the latest edition, the one most useful for this purpose.

Assuming you have generated a good, short list of perhaps four or five prospects, you now need to so some screening in person. Never hire a local lawyer without meeting him or her personally, not at lunch or at the zoo, but in his/her office. You want to determine whether this is the right person to handle an important legal matter for you. You'll need all the sensory data you can get. The telephone isn't enough. Lawyers are highly verbal and glib. They are gifted at disguising their limitations when conversing with clients. This ability is as much a part of their stock in trade as flour, tobacco or gingham that of a general store.

Call the lawyers on your list and arrange to see them, not to seek their advice, but for a brief, initial meeting on a legal matter. Mentioning that Professor Hanna or somebody else suggested you call will facilitate setting up the meeting. Some lawyers charge a fee for this brief conference. I prefer not to pay for shopping if I don't buy something. If you are like-minded, make this clear in the initial call. A professional person's time is valuable but so is everybody's and most people don't charge a fee for shopping. You're not seeking free legal advice. You're only trying to determine whether this is the person you want to hire.

"I have a matter involving a corporate pension trust. As we've never met, I'd like to have an opportunity to come and see you. Is there a fee for this introductory meeting?"

If there is, you may tell the lawyer in candor that the professor also recommended one or two other good lawyers and, other things being equal, you'd prefer not to pay this fee if that's acceptable. This puts the forces of competition to work for you. If the fee isn't waived, you must decide whether or not to pay it. My personal preference is to pass, not so much in order to save $50 or $75 or so, but because the practitioner has failed to respond accommodatingly on a matter that might easily have gone in my favor. It has the feel of somebody who is money, not service, oriented, coupled, perhaps, with a power factor I don't like and don't work with best. This sort of person tends to decide what's best for a client and implement or impose it without sufficient consultation. I would move to the next name on my list, even (especially) if, by my balking, the lawyer belatedly waived the fee, because I also don't need a lawyer who likes to play poker with a client in this way.

When you arrive for the initial meeting (on time), note what the office looks like, where it's located and how it's run. At today's prices, a good, experienced lawyer should be doing well and ought to have an appropriate front. You're not necessarily looking for a Hollywood set of how a successful firm's office should look, but a seedy, rundown office in the low-rent district won't impress you favorably.

Was it difficult to arrange the appointment? Did the lawyer try to prevent it in favor of a brief telephone conversation? Discern the lawyer's manner. Open hostility toward prospective new business is rare but look more deeply. Does he/she repeatedly interrupt you with the answer even before you've fully stated the question? This is impatience and it's a bad sign. How does this person relate to his/her secretary, colleagues and to calls taken while you're there? What are the calls about? Listen to them carefully. If you detect impatience, indifference, defensiveness, pointless conversation initiated by the lawyer, inconsiderateness, rudeness and especially lack of preparation or a lack of diligence, beware. These are auguries of real problems ahead.

A lawyer with whom you will have a good relationship and happy outcomes should be calm. I don't care how many certificates adorn the walls; if the lawyer isn't calm and calming, walk out. An erratic, frenzied lawyer is unsure, ill prepared or will attempt to force his/her views on you and everybody else. This will produce upset and friction, raise temperatures and costs, and you are likely to get an unsatisfactory result, if, indeed, you get any finished work product. The cost, not only in money, will be exorbitant in relation to the benefits. This kind of lawyer is a menace, especially in negotiations and litigations.

Look for signs of thorough preparation. This, not the lucky break at the last moment granted Perry Mason by his writers, is the key to the successful handling of legal matters, assuming the practitioner has the necessary competence. Evidence of good preparation includes a busy, ample staff of secretaries and paraprofessionals, word processors and other technological aids, lots of filing cabinets and an air of purposeful work being done calmly and neatly. If you see loose files spilling out of their folders or piled in a haphazard heap, or you notice an overturned can of Tab (or Styrofoam cup of coffee) staining a ream of papers littering the lawyer's desk and running off onto the floor, you're in the company of an ill-prepared procrastinator. Be brief and leave, taking care to leave nothing of yours in this person's possession. At a safe remove, delete this person's name from your list.

If you've assembled a good list, at least a couple of the four or five lawyers should suit you. These will have passed all of the above tests. You will also have a certain rapport with these couple of professionals, as well as confidence and trust in them.

Ask how the lawyer would approach your matter. You're not looking for free legal advice. You are trying to discover whether you and the lawyer think alike about the handling of your legal matter. If you don't, ask for an explanation. "Why do you say that, Mr./Ms. Baxendale?" Smile. You will appear less argumentative and are more likely to get a responsive answer.

If you thought, for example, the contract dispute you were having could have been handled in a couple of meetings with the lawyers for the other side but this lawyer is describing how he/she intends to bombard them with legal papers, you've got a problem. This confrontational approach may actually help the other side by delaying the result you want. Paper bombardments also cost money.

Show some respect for the lawyer's time by not wasting it in this initial meeting. You are also being evaluated. Summarize inessential details and have a short, written list of questions. The last question should be "Is there an important question I've omitted?" Once you are satisfied that this particular lawyer is the one to handle this particular legal matter for you, there is the important question of fees.

No fee arrangement with a lawyer is perfect and all may be taken advantage of by an unscrupulous practitioner. However, a client can make some intelligent choices and fees *are* negotiable. First, there has not been a minimum fee upon which the lawyer may insist since 1975, when the United States Supreme Court struck them down. Additionally, the United States Commerce Department estimates that by the year 2000 there will be 1,000,000 lawyers in this country, an oversupply or glut by anybody's definition, even in this, the most litigious society on the planet. The current ratio of one lawyer for every four hundred people in the general population (the highest on earth) will become even more lopsided. When this reality gets the publicity it deserves, lawyers (whose incivilities to clients have become commonplace) will be enrolling in "charm schools" by the long ton. Outrageous bills, usually presented on high-quality, engraved letterheads, will no doubt become more modishly sleek and streamlined. Until this millennium arrives, be sure to negotiate *all* fees with *all* lawyers unless you don't mind wasting large sums of money.

Lawyers are paid for their services in several different ways. Already mentioned is the *flat fee*. The lawyer receives an agreed sum to produce a desired result. Routine, uncomplicated matters, such as drafting a simple will or contract or the incorporation of a small business lend themselves to a flat fee. Here, the best method for keeping the flat fee reasonable is comparison shopping among legal clinics. You may select one of these clinics for this simple piece of work or give your non-clinic lawyer the results of your shopping and ask for a competitive offer.

"I can get this work done at Dombey and Son in two weeks for $250. Would you be willing to compete with that?"

You may then hear about the highly individualized services you will obtain from this highly qualified professional who cares about you in a continuing relationship, and a somewhat higher flat fee, with no mention of a delivery date. If you like the price and the lawyer, buy it (subject to a reasonable, specified delivery time), keep shopping or hire the clinic.

In every case, as will be underlined below, be sure to enter into a signed, written agreement with your lawyer. The flat fee agreement should have no loopholes in it that permit the lawyer to decide later that unforeseen complications arose that demand more legal time, and hence more of your money. Your lawyer was in a better position than you to assess this when the agreement was signed and should be held to it unless you have changed the nature of the assignment, in which case the lawyer has a right to renegotiate. In that event, you may be willing to increase the flat fee somewhat but you must insist there be no open-ended billing for time.

Other kinds of legal work are done on a *percentage* basis. A lawyer who probates a will or closes title to a house you buy or who is an executor of an estate usually gets a percentage of the amount involved. If the sums are large, the lawyer's percentage should be scaled down to reflect reasonable payment for services. A $500,000 house is as easy to "close" as a $100,000 house and shouldn't cost five times the fee. Where the percentage is not fixed by law, you should work out a sliding scale that lowers the percentage as the amounts rise, or try for a reasonable flat fee even if the lawyer tells you a percentage is customary. Remember, there are many lawyers who can handle these easy jobs and the number is rising.

A *contingent fee* is an agreed percentage to be paid only out of money you receive. If you don't receive anything, there is no fee payable. This is a common arrangement for plaintiffs in personal injury lawsuits. A plaintiff often cannot afford to pay a strong litigator on any other basis. The first-rate litigator can estimate the recovery and decide whether it's a sufficiently attractive case to accept. In a negligence case, the typical contingent fee arrangement would give the lawyer about one third, the client about two thirds, with costs and disbursements coming off the top (reimbursed out of the total recovery before the division of the balance is made), *not* all paid by you after the division is made. This gives the lawyer one third of the *net* recovery, a much more reasonable arrangement for you and one you can probably insist on with virtually every negligence lawyer, if you have a good case. As good and bad lawyers take roughly the same percentage of the contingent fee, it is extremely important that you hire an excellent litigator or you will receive less than you deserve, and perhaps nothing at all. Also, the sooner you consult a first-rate lawyer, the better prepared your case will be.

A contingent fee theoretically gives the lawyer an incentive to do a good job as he/she shares the dollars received on an agreed basis. Some lawyers will ask for a retainer to be subtracted from their share of the contingent fee. Don't pay such retainers in negligence cases. First, it isn't necessary or customary. Second, whether you have the money to pay or will borrow it, you're losing interest. Third, what if you lose? The retainer is out the window and you have no recovery to subtract it from. If a contingent fee provides an incentive to a lawyer because he/she shares in the recovery, a retainer may be said to provide a disincentive because the lawyer is paid win or lose. Don't pay it in negligence cases; and in other cases, if a retainer is absolutely necessary (where you are a plaintiff in a nonnegligence case and the lawyer you want insists), keep it as low as possible. My preference is to pay no legal fees at all if I am a plaintiff in any case and don't recover. As will be seen below, this is a negotiable point with me in some cases, but not in negligence cases.

The contingent fee arrangement is a good one if: (1) you hire a first-rate lawyer for the particular kind and size case you have; (2) you avoid the possible conflict of interest between you and your lawyer, as explained below; and (3) you and your lawyer are well prepared. The first-rate lawyer is a litigation specialist in your type of case who has won several extremely large verdicts in the precise kind of case you have and is either personally meticulous in preparing such a case for trial or has at hand other people in the firm who are.

Every large city has a handful of these professionals and it's a blessing to be able to retain one of them. *Absolutely crucial, however, is that your signed, written agreement with this lawyer unequivocally states that this lawyer will personally try the case if it goes to trial.* You don't want to be surprised on the eve of trial with the news that your lawyer is involved in another case or whatever and is therefore unavailable but that Harry or Harriet "is just as good, probably even better with your particular trial judge, and he (or she) is completely prepared to try your case." Get a postponement, faint dead away on the floor, but under no circumstances permit Harry or Harriet to try your case. This is totally unacceptable and you may show the person suggesting it a photocopy (not the original) of the agreement your lawyer signed. The only possible excuse you should be willing to consider for your lawyer's not trying the case is death, and then only seldom.

The conflict of interest to be avoided, referred to earlier, comes in one of a couple of versions. In version one, the case goes sour or the lawyer loses interest in it for some other reason, usually involving the need for too much work, the prospect of too small a recovery or the fact that a much bigger case has captured his/her attention. This version assumes that your lawyer was a good choice initially, except for this character flaw. In other words, the essential competence was and is there but the motivation has disappeared. If you made the mistake of choosing the wrong lawyer, then you've got version two of the conflict of interest. Your lawyer is unable to compete effectively in a trial setting and expected the case to be settled before trial.

In all of the above cases, the lawyer wants to settle your case as soon as possible, pocket his/her share of the proceeds and move on to some other income-producing pursuit. However, you may not be willing to accept the settlement offer (which is your right). You prefer a trial. A reluctant or incompetent lawyer is not somebody likely to get a great result in a courtroom and you may expect delays (without much, if any, work product), excuses and a strong sales presentation on the subject of why you should accept the settlement offer, followed by a bad, perhaps disastrous, handling of the trial if you refuse. You would probably do better either to hire somebody else (see firing your lawyer, below) if you have a good case that's still viable, or to pour your joint energies into negotiating a better settlement (if your lawyer's eagerness to settle hasn't scotched this possibility) when the conflict of interest emerges. The settlement problem, however, will most likely have been complicated by your lawyer's all too obvious (to the other side) lost taste for a trial. If you've committed your lawyer in writing to try the case personally, as suggested, and your lawyer refuses to do so, you *may* have grounds that constitute breach of contract. If so, this would entitle your lawyer to nothing of the contingent fee (making it easy to negotiate him/her out of the case for something small or the promise of same) and facilitate your hiring another lawyer to try the case. Ordinarily, when you exercise the right to fire your lawyer, he or she has a lien on the case.

The other common cost basis for legal services is for *time*. You pay by the hour for the time spent on your legal matter. Billing rates vary within the firm and several different people may be working on different parts of your matter. A senior partner's time in a major firm might cost $200 per hour; that of a junior partner, perhaps $125; an associate, say $85, and a paralegal, maybe $25 or $30.

As the time sheets are completely controlled by the seller, it's impossible to assure that your bill will be accurate. You don't know who is doing the actual work so a paralegal's time may appear on your bill as that of a senior partner. Even if there is no intention to overcharge, few people work uninterruptedly for several hours at a time but they tend to bill as if they do. Telephone calls, coffee breaks, rest-room breaks, unrelated conversations with colleagues may easily not be subtracted from the time "spent" on your matter. If your lawyer or anybody working on your matter leaves the office, you are billed door to door. If your lawyer travels out of town, you are normally billed all of the travel time plus seven or so hours per day regardless of the time spent on your matter. Often, if more than one client is being serviced, they are each billed for full time spent.

Then, too, there is no incentive to be economical of time. You may thus be paying for oversights, dishonesty and inefficiency. You may also be paying for the education of your lawyer in that somebody not well versed in the intricacies of the law governing your matter or unskilled in the handling of it may spend much time learning, all of which winds up on your time sheets.

Other extraneous factors can also run up your bill needlessly. A cantankerous counselor, a balky defendant or a lawyer on the other side who is also being paid on an hourly basis and may therefore engage in much make-work (causing your side to waste time responding), all are charged to you if you pay by the hour. If you don't have "deep pockets," the other side may exert undue pressure on you by deliberately and intentionally forcing your lawyer to waste much time in order to weaken your hold on your case as the costs mount. Thus, payment on the basis of time is expensive, uncontrolled and fraught with disadvantages and pitfalls.

Often, the lawyer you want to hire will tell you the *firm* insists on hourly billings. I have met that objection by suggesting that the firm be paid its hourly rates but that a "cap" be put on this amount. The cap is a maximum figure, beyond which you pay no more legal fees. If this principle is accepted and the cap is a reasonable amount, well and good; you're out of the hourly billing trap. If not, I have prevailed over open-ended hourly billing rates with the following structure: hourly billing rates up to a (reasonably small) cap, against a percentage of the recovery.

This works as follows. Say, for example, you're a plaintiff in a non-negligence litigation. Say it's a commercial case. You think that with good lawyering the case might be worth between $100,000 and $200,000. You know that if you pay straight hourly rates you have no control over the fees. If it goes all the way through trial (and maybe even an appeal), it may cost as much or more in fees as you recover, if you win. If you lose, it's a double disaster of big fees and no recovery. You also don't want to permit the other side to pressure you with the legal cost (to you) of their delays. (Defendants are in no rush. It's a trial they're going to, not a vacation.)

You've selected an excellent lawyer who, if he/she likes your case, may well accept hourly billings up to, say, a maximum of $15,000 or $20,000 (the cap) all of which will be credited against, say, one third of your recovery if you go through trial and one fourth if the case is settled earlier, with some small additional fee if one or the other side appeals. Thus, if you settle the case prior to a verdict for $120,000, the lawyer gets a total fee of $30,000. If you recover $150,000 after a trial, with no appeal, the fee is $50,000. If you lose the case, the fee is the hourly billings, up to a maximum of $15,000. If your case involves a much larger amount of money, I would also try to structure a sliding scale that reduces the lawyer's percentage as the amounts of the potential recovery rise.

The American Bar Association suggests a written fee agreement, stating the basis on which you will be charged, be entered into before the lawyer does "substantial" work on a matter. This is a must. It might be wise to consult another lawyer for advice about this agreement before you sign it. You should require monthly interim bills in order to prevent any undue surprises. If litigation or negotiation is involved, be especially careful about getting a written commitment as to who will do the work. Don't sign the agreement until you understand every word of it. There are, for example, words like "reasonable" in some of these agreements that mean anything but that for you. In addition to charging high hourly (or other) fees, lawyers nonchalantly add to these costs in ways undreamed of by ordinary civilians but which are sanctioned by the Lawyers' Code of Professional Responsibility.

This code, for example, sanctions payment to a lawyer over and above hourly billing rates for such items as the difficulty of the work, the speed with which it is done, the amounts others charge for similar services, the reputation of the law firm, whether working for you precludes working for somebody else and a number of other considerations that are rarely, if ever, itemized, including "the value of the transaction." The usual bill for legal services for which you are paying hourly rates typically arrives without the slightest indication of how many hours of work were involved or who did the work. Obviously, if a clerk photocopied some papers or a typist typed some material, this time should not be billed at the same rate as that of the lawyer. In addition, there may have been several junior lawyers working on your case at substantially lower rates than that set for the lawyer you hired.

Do not, therefore, commit yourself to pay "reasonable" fees. It's also a good idea to learn how to complain effectively about overbilling. In an article written by Dan Lewolt in the fifth anniversary edition of the H.A.L.T. newspaper (Help Abolish Legal Tyranny, 201 Massachusetts Avenue N.E.,

Washington, D.C. 20002), he reports that a complaining member consulted with a H.A.L.T. staff attorney about a $34,000 bill for legal services "connected with the exchange of valuable properties." At the lawyer's $125 hourly rate and without disputing the lawyer's own time sheets, the fee should have been about $14,000.

Upon inquiry, the lawyer explained that the additional $20,000 "was based on the value of the transaction." H.A.L.T.'s staff attorney advised the complaining member that in most jurisdiction, in the absence of a written fee agreement, the "reasonable fee provision" of the Code of Professional Responsibility permitting this add-on is usually decisive. Therefore, if the matter were litigated, the client would have the burden of proving an implied or expressed agreement to work for hourly rates only.

The alternative suggested by H.A.L.T. was a letter from the client to the firm demonstrating the former's reasonableness and flexibility but stating clearly that he'd never agreed to pay "reasonable" fees based on a definition of which he'd been unaware; that he'd never agreed to pay on the basis of the "value of the transaction"; and that much of what the firm seemed to be billing for was already included in the hourly fees. The member agreed to accept the hours as itemized and to pay the highest amount mentioned by the lawyer —namely, $125 per hour. Bottom line: the firm accepted $14,000 as payment in full.

Stay in close touch with your legal matter and your lawyer. Ask to receive a copy of every piece of paper in the file on a continuing basis, even if you are charged a photocopying fee. Keep a file on your own case. If you don't hear from your lawyer at least a couple of times a month, call him/her. Keep a log on the communication between you and the lawyer so you may see where the snags occur and determine whether your matter is being neglected. You should be consulted before any of the lawyer's decisions is implemented. You have a right to make decisions on your matter and should do so after the lawyer explains the alternatives.

You also have the right to fire your lawyer. If you do so, you will be liable for the reasonable value of the lawyer's services at the time you fire him/her *unless* you have "good cause." Good cause is difficult to establish but, in general, it involves dishonesty, incompetence or a pattern of neglect in the handling of your matter. The practical problems in firing a lawyer involve the difficulties in substituting a good lawyer for the fired one, establishing how each will be paid, getting the file to the second lawyer and the delay and likely slippage in getting the new lawyer up to speed in the matter.

Lawyers are the most maligned professionals in the world, not without much justification. However, if you choose wisely and keep both hands on the reins, your chances for being a satisfied client are at least pretty good, and for avoiding a host of all too common problems, excellent.

☐ Health Care

A generation ago, the medical profession was generally thought to be populated by kindly, omniscient types exclusively dedicated to the well-being of their patients. In the face of a plethora of P.C.'s, extensive media coverage of nursing-home scandals, falsified drug research, malpractice suits and the unvarnished evidence provided by a number of medical mavericks, this notion has been abandoned by large segments of the better informed. Then, too, although the word "iatrogenic" (maladies and diseases caused by the diagnosis, manner or treatment of a physician or surgeon) hasn't yet appeared in a *TV Guide* crossword puzzle, it has gained considerable currency. As good health care is important and costs a lot of money (more than 10 percent of the U.S. gross national product), it's certainly worth considering how to get maximum value with an absolute minimum of upset.

When you visit a doctor, you are at a number of positional disadvantages. The doctor is presumably well, while you or a loved one accompanying you is ill or in need of a checkup that may reveal illness. The doctor has special knowledge and education you don't have and a number of credentials on the wall that emphasize this point. The doctor has learned a specialized language you don't fully understand which can be used at will to underscore the doctor's knowledge and your ignorance. The doctor is fully clothed and often appears in a white, laboratory coat; you are, or recently were, undressed. You have come for the doctor's help to the doctor's office at the doctor's convenience and you've waited while other patients were called into an inner chamber to receive benefits from this learned professional. You will also see the doctor control much expensive equipment and perform or order additional tests and you will pay for these services so they must be valuable.

In view of all of this stage management, set decoration, costuming, lighting and other preparations usually associated with the dramatic arts, is it any wonder patients willingly suspend disbelief in their dealings with doctors? The patient's complacency and his desire to avoid responsibility add to the effect of ascribing a kind of omniscience to the doctor that tends to feed on itself and may be harmful to the patient's health.

You are presumably not seeking a religious experience at the doctor's office so a healthy skepticism will stand you in good stead if you are careful not to offend the doctor. Not every practitioner is an expert diagnostician, and mistaken diagnoses, both of omission and commission, are not uncommon. Unless you are faced with a medical emergency, second and third opinions are advisable before you resort to any radical measures.

I recently heard of a case that involved a woman jogger for whom a doctor recommended knee surgery. Fortunately, this woman had the good sense to seek a second opinion, this time from a specialist in sports medicine. It turned out her feet were out of balance and an orthotic device was prescribed. The woman jogs as much as ever and her knees are perfectly normal without surgery.

Many doctors tend to overprescribe drugs. As patients are apt to feel either shortchanged or that their symptoms are not being taken seriously unless their doctor writes out a prescription, the doctor is happy to cooperate. Most of the information your doctor has about modern prescription drugs comes from the drug companies that manufacture them, via advertisements in medical magazines and the company's sales force, the latter known as "medical detailers." This should raise your threshold of skepticism. Ask questions.

"Are there any side effects or contraindications I should be aware of, Doctor?"

Speak slowly. Look directly at the doctor. Wait for an answer and decide how seriously the doctor seems to be taking this question. Note whether you get a prompt, direct answer. All drugs are invasive of your body and all cause side effects. What *are* the side effects and other risks in this particular one? Is there a safer alternative? What would happen if you didn't take the drug? May you see the package insert that comes with the drug (that lists side effects and other risks)? Are there any contraindications for the drug? Is there something you should be aware of if you take the drug that will suggest you *stop* taking it? You should also be sure to tell the doctor about all the other drugs you may be taking as the prescribed drug may interact with such drugs in ways harmful to you.

Don't stop there. Do some further checking. Most public libraries have reference copies of the *Physicians' Desk Reference,* known as the PDR, which clearly sets forth the side effects of drugs. You may also want to consult the *Drug Evaluations* book published by the American Medical Association. There is a handy index of symptoms in the back of this book that refers to the drugs that produce them. These books are also obtainable at medical bookstores.

Diagnostic testing is by no means conclusive. The equipment may be defective, the test may have been administered improperly or the results misinterpreted. Even the test itself may be ill-conceived. A lawyer friend of mine, who is usually fairly hardheaded, consulted a doctor who recommended that a blood sample be tested for allergies to various foods and other substances. The doctor just happened to have the sophisticated, computerized testing equipment in his office for administering and evaluating the test.

The test was taken and the results duly printed out, at a cost to my friend of about $200. The doctor then discussed the results and cautioned my friend to avoid the foods and substances to which he had been "found" allergic.

"How can I avoid things like household dust? It's everywhere. What about a cure?"

The doctor was not optimistic.

"How accurate is this test?" my friend belatedly asked.

"About 50 percent."

"I wish I had known that I could have gotten equally valid 'information' by tossing a coin before I took the test."

My friend wrote off the $200 and the doctor.

EKGs, EEGs, X rays and other diagnostic tests are subject to mechanical error, malfunction and misinterpretation, and laboratory tests have been found to be similarly unreliable. The same samples submitted to a dozen laboratories are likely to yield a wide spectrum of test results. Unless you find yourself in an emergency or extremely high risk situation in which even the slightest delay could be dangerous, it would seem prudent to retest adverse results before accepting the diagnosis or the suggested corrective measures that accompany it. The retesting should be done on different diagnostic equipment or by a different laboratory with a good reputation. A second medical opinion should come from a doctor who has a different hospital affiliation than the first doctor. This helps avoid self-fulfilling prophecies about your health.

Many patients, especially some women, tend to idealize their doctors. They are inclined to follow instructions without sufficient explanation. Ask questions. Get a specific diagnosis. Share in the management of your health by learning about the condition diagnosed. It isn't beyond your ability. You can learn a great deal about a specific condition. There are excellent medical libraries available to the general public. You have access to treatises, textbooks and other medical works as well as valuable translations of medical journals published in dozens of other countries. The latest studies are thus within your reach. A librarian will assist you and even arrange to photocopy the material you request at a nominal cost. An intelligent patient can and should take an active role in the process. The time I spent at the New York Academy of Medicine may have saved my life.

Without going into all the uninspiring details, my (then) physician completely overlooked a node I had growing out of the side of my thyroid gland, despite a "complete" physical examination for which he'd charged $140 in 1964 dollars. When I later discovered it and called it to his attention, he dismissed it as "insignificant." By this time I'd had an opportunity to learn something about thyroid nodes and to discover that I was in the highest category of risk: a single node in a male patient under forty. I insisted on seeing a specialist.

The doctor the physician recommended, and whose credentials I scrutinized, was the chief thyroid therapist of an important hospital and had specialized in this field for thirty-seven years. This doctor suggested a course of treatment with thyroid hormone and did certain tests (a radioactive iodine scan and uptake), the results of which looked normal to him (and to me). I got eight other "second" opinions from other respected physicians and surgeons, whose opinions were divided along the lines of their specialties. The surgeons recommended immediate surgery; those versed in pharmacology thought drugs might be beneficial, and so on.

A year later I repeated the scan and uptake with the thyroid therapist and was told I was in the normal range. I disagreed, pointed out that if he compared the two scans side by side (which he'd failed to do) he would notice evidence of minor changes. Coupled with the low uptake and the fact I was in the highest risk category, surgery, I told him, was clearly indicated. He did the comparison and recommended surgery.

The doctor who'd failed to discover the node and had dismissed it as insignificant misinformed my family and me that the node was benign but I realized from the medication that I either had thyroid cancer or a darned good malpractice suit against the surgeon. I asked a lawyer friend to resolve this question by getting a copy of every page of the hospital record and the truth, thyroid cancer, was evident. I cite the case because I think it is extremely important that you do not simply give yourself over to the care of a doctor, however competent and well intentioned the practitioner may be. You have the greatest stake in the outcome and must assume a large and continuing role in the decision-making that affects your health.

Not always honest or forthright, many doctors are also careless with their patients' time. No doubt you've had the unpleasant experience of sitting in a doctor's waiting room for an hour or two, surrounded by other waiting patients, some of whom probably had communicable diseases. What can you do about it? There are a number of ways you can emphasize the value of your time and raise the level of respect for punctuality with which the doctor's office treats you. Several years ago, I suggested the following approach.

After you've arrived on time and waited about ten minutes, walk over to the secretary or receptionist.

"Excuse me. My name is ———. I have a two o'clock appointment and it's getting a bit late. When may I see the doctor?"

Delivered politely and unobtrusively, this request may create a preference for you but will more often than not elicit the response that others are similarly situated, that the doctor is doing his/her best, but that an unexpected emergency upset the schedule. This explanation is probably false. The doctor doesn't want to have to wait for the next patient as this reduces the amount of billable time and the number of patients who can be seen per day. Therefore, on the principle that the doctor's time is precious and the patient's of little value and no concern (with a few exceptions for the heavyweight clients you may occasionally see being led into an inner office immediately upon arrival), the doctor, with the help of the staff, simply overbooks each day, allowing enough time toward the close of business to empty the office and leave at about the usual hour. The doctor is thus able to come and go on time and bill out the entire day without any unproductive gaps while hundreds of patients are kept waiting each week. Some of these doctors even have the temerity to bill a patient who cancels without "sufficient" notice. If you want to test the good faith of the "emergency" excuse, cast your eye over the doctor's schedule for the day. If you see the close of the day relatively lightly scheduled, you may take this as evidence of an uncaring doctor about the value of your time.

What I suggested in other books and in the electronic media was that if you had to wait the hour and a half or two, when the doctor's bill for, say, $35 arrived, you bill the doctor for two hours of waiting time at a nominal $25 per hour, for a total of $50, directly on the doctor's bill. Then, give the doctor a $15 professional discount, substract your $35 from the doctor's $35 for a balance due of zero and return the *original* bill the doctor sent you (raising the anxiety level in the doctor's office about your payment of the doctor's bill).

This approach was intended to make the point that the patient's time also has a value to be respected, not as a means of evading payment. Thus, when the anticipated telephone call comes from the doctor's secretary, I would relent by expressing my willingness to pay the bill, but only on the understanding that the next time I arrive on time, in the absence of some real and rare emergency, I would be able to see the doctor with reasonable promptness. This usually produces the desired effect.

It's often desirable to have somebody other than you make your appointments with doctors. A friend, neighbor or colleague who speaks with a little authority can make an important difference, especially for (some) women who, all too often, are still given less than equal treatment, even by other women. Your willingness to reciprocate should be sufficient inducement.

"I'm Susan Miller calling for Edna Breen."

This interposition of a third person not only enhances your status in the mind of the doctor's secretary, but it also requires the latter to deal with somebody with limited authority, thus reducing your side's flexibility. As your agent may not readily rearrange your schedule to accommodate the other side, the doctor's office is constrained to do the accommodating. By suggesting a number of possible times for the appointment, all preselected by you, your agent is seen as cooperative. The other person is moved to cooperate by picking the first matching time available, or even arranging to "squeeze Ms. Breen in" under the circumstances.

For best results, on the day of the appointment, have somebody call to confirm an hour or so in advance.

"I'm confirming Ms. Breen's appointment with Dr. Rosenzweig for two o'clock today. She's booked rather tightly so we're checking to be sure the doctor will be able to see her as scheduled."

This emphasizes the value of your time and raises the level of respect others will have for it. If you'd prefer to take your chances on your doctor's fidelity to your appointment without these scheduling aids, you might be well advised to take a rotisserie and be prepared to camp out in the doctor's office.

Look for other ways to get full value from these appointments. Make up a list of questions and symptoms for the doctor to consider. If you think the doctor is not giving your questions enough serious thought, you may add weight to them by including a family member, loved one or friend as a reference.

"Bill and I are particularly interested in your opinion about these dizzy spells I've been having lately, Doctor."

A similar effect may be created by having somebody accompany you in the doctor's study. This is particularly important in conversations with surgeons. Your relationship with a particular surgeon is usually not a long one but it is an important one. In order to raise the degree of certainty the surgeon you have selected will perform the actual surgery it's a good idea to have somebody close to you present in the surgeon's office when you seek assurance on this point.

"We want to be sure that you will perform the operation, Dr. Sherman."

You would like to avoid an operation "ghosted" by the surgeon's apt protégé in need of on-the-job training.

The relationship between you and your doctor may become strained. Happily, the licensing body is a handy tool easily interposed on these occasions. Many an arrogant professional will choose to back off from the avoidable paperwork and the needless jeopardies of a grievance procedure before the duly constituted licensing body.

I once needed the services of an ear, nose and throat specialist while my doctor was recuperating from a stroke. He used an old-fashioned but extremely effective piece of equipment that pumped out the products of the infection from the sinuses and nature then provided the cure. It was simple, effective, worked every time for me and there were no drugs with their side effects.

My doctor's office didn't know of anybody else who used this equipment. However, after a few calls, I found a specialist whose secretary assured me her employer had the equipment and could administer the treatment I sought. To make sure, I waited on the line while this was confirmed. I made an appointment.

After being kept waiting for about two hours, the doctor told me he did not have the equipment nor did he do the procedure and he further informed me that he, not the patient, would decide how to treat the patient. I pointed out that had I not been misinformed I wouldn't have been "treated" to a two-hour wait and told him I would require nothing further from him, including the processing of the throat culture he'd taken, and made it clear I would not pay anything for the so-called visit. As I was leaving, the secretary called after me:

"Mr. Charell!"

"Yes."

"That's $65."

"Send me a bill."

"We don't send bills."

"Then don't send me a bill," I said, leaving.

Later that day, I called the doctor's secretary, told her not to send the throat culture to the laboratory as I wouldn't pay for it, informed her that the doctor did not have the equipment nor did he do the procedure we'd discussed earlier, contrary to what she'd told me, and that I therefore would not pay for the visit. When the bill for $65 arrived, I called the New York County Medical Society. Without mentioning the doctor's name, I discussed the propriety of the bill with the executive secretary. I was advised to write a complaint letter to the grievance committee.

I finessed that by going to the next level and was able to reach a doctor on the board of ethics who agreed with me and gave me permission to quote him by name. In one more call to the doctor's secretary, I did precisely that and made it clear that if I ever received another bill or heard anything further about the matter, I would file a formal complaint with the grievance committee, as advised by the executive secretary. The doctor decided not to press it.

The general shopping suggestions for choosing a professional apply to selecting a good family doctor, general practitioner, and internist. In addition, look at your prospective doctor's hospital affiliations. If I faced a condition serious enough to require hospitalization, I would want the best care available in the area. Affiliations with the best hospitals also gives you easy access to the specialists and surgeons associated with these hospitals, your doctor's colleagues, and they are also presumably first-rate or at least darned good.

The doctor-patient relationship is a highly personal one and personal relationships often change their character over the course of time for a variety of reasons. Your doctor may no longer have the energy or inclination to meet all of your needs or may be thinking of retiring and not be keeping up with developments in the field. Your own needs may have changed to the point that you would be better served by a different doctor. If so, be strong enough to overcome inertia and find a more suitable professional.

Look for somebody who fits your special needs and preferences. I like to be kept fully informed by doctors and to take an active role in my own health care. Some doctors still prefer to play God and are ill suited for the role. I would rather have less self-styled omniscience and more communication. It's also important that your doctor keep abreast of developments in his/her field. My preference here is for a doctor close to the middle of his/her practicing years. This gives me much experience coupled with good energy and a desire to stay well prepared.

Many of the major cities in this country have magazines available that bear the city's name and have probably done at least one article on the subject of the "best" professionals in their various fields. This is worth a telephone call to the library of the magazine if you live in an area in which this might apply. Don't stop there. Ask professionals in other fields whose work you respect to recommend a doctor if they're satisfied and if you think you have similar needs. By this I mean, if you are biased in favor of noninvasive care, you may or may not get this sort of care if you're doctor is a Ph.D. in pharmacology. The time to meet with prospective doctors is early on, before your need is acute, so that you have the luxury of being able to choose carefully without incurring major risks.

Surgery and hospitalization are big-ticket expenses with consequences that go far beyond their considerable costs. Assuring your satisfaction with surgeons and hospitals requires preparation and attention to details. First, there is the consideration of insurance. I don't espouse overinsurance but major medical coverage is a must. If you think you can't afford it, ask about the rates with higher deductibles. The differences in costs between coverage of, say, $250,000 with a $100 or $200 annual deductible and the same policy with a deductible of $500 or a $1,000 might well make the difference between buying the insurance and being wiped out financially by a catastrophic illness.

If you are presently covered but may have to cancel on account of cost, you can easily arrange a higher deductible with correspondingly lower cost. The insurance company is almost always willing to negotiate a lower liability for itself. Group coverage can also lower costs and absorb risks that might not be acceptable to the company on an individual basis. If you've ever been refused such a policy or think you might be, a good broker can steer you past this barrier, if not at one time, then by degrees over time. This usually requires perhaps a waiver of certain claims and/or a higher rate the first year with these being stripped away progressively each year until you may have a policy standard in every respect.

In-hospital nursing care supplied by the hospital varies in quality over an astonishing range. I would guess that 99 percent of patients accept the luck of the draw when they may easily be able to arrange to get the services of Florence Nightingale and avoid the Marquis de Sade. This will probably be denied but in most first-rate hospitals there is usually a VIP wing or at least a couple of VIP floors (often the top two floors, not unlike the tower floors of a hotel). The rich and famous are routinely housed in this wing or on these floors. Many of these patients hire their own private nurses twenty-four hours a day. This frees the hospital's nursing staff to take better care of the other patients on these floors. Staff morale is much higher on these floors. Proximity to money and celebrity has this effect and the lighter work load adds to it. As a result, patients on these floors get much more for their money and they get it with a smile.

Your hospital nurse is the only health-care professional

who has twenty-four-hour responsibility for you while you are in the hospital. There are times, especially during the night shift, when the nursing staff is thin and overworked. Most hospital deaths (particularly the needless ones) occur on this shift. Getting a room on the VIP floors will not only make your stay more pleasant and thus aid recovery, it may even save your life.

There is an additional benefit. Insurance companies usually pay in full for semiprivate room charges, with the patient paying the difference for a private room. This differential involves from several hundred to thousands of dollars in a typical hospitalization and you may therefore opt for semiprivate. However, semiprivate is a nonspecific designation that may mean one other patient shares your room or as many as five. Here, again, the VIP floors offer the best odds.

How do you get VIP treatment? One way is to explain your preference to your doctor and surgeon. Point out your particular sensitivity to environmental stimuli and how much of a difference this will mean to your health. Not too many civilians even know such a preference exists so there's not too much demand for it. Have somebody with you who will support your request. This will strengthen your chances of being satisfied.

If possible, visit the hospital before you check in. Talk to the patients on several floors as they stroll about. Ask how they like the nursing care and the food. Ask their friends and relatives the same questions as they wait for the descending elevator or while they are in the lounge. Get the feel of the place.

Your surgeon may well have affiliations at more than one hospital. You may even look at those hospitals if you are displeased with the one reserved for you. The unavailability of a bed may present a problem if there is a pressing need for the operation, but I wouldn't rule out the possibility and might well make the case with my surgeon if the surgery could be postponed without adding to the risks. If you can't visit the hospital in advance, perhaps an intelligent, sensitive friend or relative would do this scouting for you. One of the criteria for selecting a hospital is its proximity to people who care about you.

Think of the hospital as an expensive hotel in which you don't have to accept an unsatisfactory accommodation. Make sure you have a functioning telephone in the room. If you are registered in an unsatisfactory room, call and make this known to your doctor and surgeon or (better still) have somebody close to you do so and conserve your energy. If all else fails, think of the hospital administrator (whose name you should get before you check in) as the manager of a hotel. Call him/her. The room is impeding your recovery. You can't sleep. You're continually awakened by noises on the floor. The staff on this floor is negligent or virtually invisible, and so on. Make it clear you need to be transferred and will be calling your doctor and surgeon if this isn't arranged at once.

Preparation, always helpful, may be crucial in this case. A small gift to your doctor's and your surgeon's receptionist or secretary prior to your hospital admission is advisable. Bath oil or toilet water for women and cologne for men are touching little gifts with your thanks and appreciation "for their help during this trying time." They cost about ten dollars or so, and as the recipients haven't done a blessed thing for you, it puts a kind of claim on them. If your doctor is unavailable to your call for help from the hospital, make your appeal to this person, who will be available during normal business hours. This person is an old hand at making requests or demands in the doctor's name and the word "doctor" carries much weight in hospitals, as in the following example.

A friend underwent hand surgery for Dupuytren's contracture. The operation was successful, the prognosis excellent. However, when I visited him one evening, he seemed uncharacteristically disconsolate. He had written out his dinner order but had received only Jell-O. When he inquired about the rest of the meal, he was told the kitchen was closed. I offered to go outside and get him anything he wanted but he refused.

"What did you order?" I asked.

"Lobster tails."

"Sounds good. Do they have that?"

"It was on the menu."

"Mind if I use your telephone?" I asked, picking up the receiver. I requested the kitchen. "This is Dr. Charell. With whom am I speaking?"

I spoke briskly, taking only a slight liberty as I do have a Juris Doctor.

"I'm with the patient in room 804. He ordered lobster tails and got Jell-O. I want him to have the lobster tails. He needs the glycogen. Send up three lobster tails with all the trimmings to 804, please, right away."

When the order arrived, my friend's face, previously tense, softened into a smile and he remained in good spirits during the entire visit, long after we finished eating.

A small point about hospital food. Many patients, particularly the elderly, don't eat the food and this weakens them. If they were served better food, better prepared, no doubt more of it would be eaten. Your surgeon, if sensitively approached in advance by you or a loved one, can arrange with the hospital dietician for you to have other than the usual fare. If you can arrange for a little special treatment on an airline meal flight in coach, why not get the best available food at hospital prices? Put the request to your surgeon in a brief, handwritten note and use capital letters.

Some of the more basic hospital patient rights include the right to personal dignity, the right of physical privacy, the right to refuse to be used for teaching or experimentation and the right to refuse treatment. Others involve your right to change doctors, the right of informed consent, the right to leave the hospital, of confidentiality and the right to access to hospital records. Some of these rights are still being tested in various parts of the country so you may not get all of them automatically in a particular case.

You may occasionally find it necessary to preserve the rights you do have. Feel free to read carefully, to discuss and to modify documents handed to you for signature in the hospital. You don't have to wait until the night before surgery, when you're under stress and alone in your hospital room. You or a friend, family member, lawyer or other concerned person should get a copy of any such document after your doctor has made the hospital reservation for you but before you check in. This will give you an opportunity to modify the document before you sign it. If you don't take this precaution and are suddenly confronted with such a document and a pen, you may request a consultation with somebody on the premises who advises patients on their rights. Question anything you don't understand or have reservations about and feel free to cross out those parts of the document to which you object. With some good management on your part, health care can actually be beneficial to your health.

☐ Travel

Business and vacation travel are expensive and even a well-planned trip may include a few unpleasant surprises. Travel time is also limited, so a bad trip has little salvage value. You can't simply scrap it and begin again. Given the high costs and built-in uncertainties, how may you reasonably expect to come home happy?

An acceptable alternative to perfection is to buy the trip that appeals to you but arrange to get more, pay less and be treated better. This combination of benefits has a relaxing, even tranquilizing effect. It's much easier for you to rise above an occasional lapse or shortcoming with smiling equanimity than it is for the similarly situated, irate guests across the dining room or down the hall who paid substantially more than you for significantly less. Live and let live.

Airline travel offers a number of opportunities. For example, have you ever seen advertisements for half-price fares coast-to-coast but the restrictions in the fine print make them unavailable to you? Say you're the man or woman who flies from New York to Los Angeles fairly regularly but you stay no more than three or four days and the half-price round trip is available only to those who make the return flight at least seven days later. You're one of the airline's best customers but the special discount is being withheld from you. There ought to be a way for you to save too. Well, there is.

Next time, buy the half-price round-trip ticket and get aboard. Say you leave New York on the fifth of the month and will be returning on the eighth. Leave the date open for your return flight. You would ordinarily be ineligible for the discount because your return flight would not be at least seven days later. However, when you arrive (or before you leave) buy a *second* half-priced ticket, this one leaving Los Angeles on the eighth with an open return date. When you return to New York on the eighth of the month, use the *first* half of the *second* ticket (Los Angeles to New York).

A couple of weeks later, when you go to Los Angeles again, use the *second* half of the *second* ticket (New York to Los Angeles). When you return three days later, use the *second* half of the *first* ticket (Los Angeles to New York). You will have flown two cross country round trips for the price of one.

Another way to save money on airline flights involves the concept of the "major" airport. A major airport is one that services extremely heavy traffic. Airlines operating out of major airports usually have a number of competitors flying similar routes operating out of the same terminal. This competition and the deregulation of the industry tend to lower the costs of flights from one major airport to another major. Thus, flights between A and B, when both A and B are major airports will almost always cost less than flights of similar distances between A and C, when C is not a major airport, or between C and D, when both C and D are not major. Prices may vary among the airlines servicing the flight from

A to B but it is fairly easy to comparison-shop the carriers flying this route and come up with the schedule and rate most suitable for you.

If you are flying from A (a major) to C (a non-major), you may save a significant amount of the fare if you divide your trip into two flights, a long flight between two majors and a short one involving a non-major. New York to Los Angeles to Tucson should be less expensive than New York to Tucson, despite the fact that the latter route is shorter. Similarly, Sacramento to Los Angeles to Boston will be less expensive than Sacramento to Boston.

With deregulation, there are about 100,000 airline fare and scheduling changes per month worldwide, so it's unrealistic to expect your travel agent or an airline reservationist to be aware of the total market. Their reluctance to do a little extra work with their computer may easily cost you money or inconvenience, or both. Do some comparison shopping. Make three or four telephone calls. Ask about connecting flights that will save you money or are at more convenient times. Ask what other airlines fly this route, what equipment will be flown, alternate routes, scheduling and prices.

Note that the lowest fare for one person may not be the lowest cost if you are traveling with another adult and some children. Some other airline may be offering a "family" fare. In addition, your travel agent may have a computerized system that is biased toward a particular airline. It may therefore require some extra work to eliminate this bias and give you the information you need in order to make an informed decision. Ask the questions suggested above and if the answers come too quickly, you have a lazy agent.

As an example of availabilities, I made some calls on November 9, 1984, and got the following information. Standard coach fare round trip, New York to Chicago, on American and United was $536. The least expensive fare on both airlines was $138. On American, the latter required advance purchase at least seven days in advance and flights after 7 P.M. or on a weekend plus at least one Saturday had to be spent in the arrival city. United had thirteen different availabilities. The $138 round trip required an advance purchase at least seven days in advance, nonstop flights after 7 P.M. Monday through Friday or any time on a Saturday or Sunday, and you had to remain until after midnight on at least one Saturday to qualify. TWA quoted a regular coach fare of $309 round trip and their lowest single round trip fare was $178. This required purchase at least seven days in advance and a stay until at least one Saturday but no restrictions on scheduling.

Hotels and car rental companies charge a surprising range of prices for the same services. One reason for this wide variation is that these services are highly perishable. They can't be stored and sold later. An unoccupied hotel room or a rental car sitting in the car renter's garage produces no revenues.

Some of this idle capacity can easily be made available to you at a cut rate. By cut rate I don't mean to imply second-rate. There is enough idle capacity at all price levels to permit you to choose among high-, medium- and low-priced services. I enjoy the amenities of deluxe hotels at moderate prices, often drive a Lincoln at less than the price of a Ford, and so on.

Say, for example, you want to stay at the Chadwick, a good commercial hotel. Call the hotel at about 10:30 P.M. local time. The day shift is off the premises; the night shift has cleared the decks and is settling in. Ask for the night manager. If you're planning to stay more than one night, keep this card facedown for the moment.

Frequent, or high-volume, users of a service usually get a discount and you'd like to receive this benefit. You're not going to misstate any facts but you intend to present yourself in a favorable light. You either stay at this hotel when you're in town or you're considering doing so.

"I (or better still, 'We") stay at the Chadwick whenever we're in town. We'll be coming in toward the middle of April. May we have the corporate rate?" Or, "We're looking for a good place to stay when we're in town. Our next trip is planned for mid-April. May we have the corporate rate?"

You may be told the corporate rate applies only to companies:

"Apply on your corporate letterhead and we'll process your request."

You now know such a discount is available, as you'd anticipated. All that remains to be done is to secure it. If you think this person can be persuaded, try this:

"Save us the paperwork and we'll be sure to pay by company check."

If you were planning to stay more than one night, play that card here. "Save us the paperwork and we'll stay two nights instead of one and we'll pay by company check."

Pause here. Don't press. Let the idea register. You'll be spending money on meals and other items at the hotel on which they also make a profit. You're not asking for the moon. Others are getting the corporate rate. You've already established that. Besides, you're going to a big city in the United States, not a desert during the monsoon season. There are several other good hotels there that will be pleased to do business with you at a discount. If the response is anything but favorable, underscore the additional profit potential your patronage represents.

"In addition to being a frequent business traveler, I also eat most of my meals in the hotel."

If this still fails to bring agreement or you're told to do something further in order to get the corporate rate, simply ask, "Don't *you* have the authority to arrange it for us *now?*" This person almost undoubtedly does have this authority because it's a fairly routine matter. I've checked out of hotels and gotten the corporate rate for the same night with no reservation in a single call to the front desk. It's not difficult.

"Somebody booked me into the Harrowing Arms for a couple of nights but I find it unsuitable." After the clerk assured me he could accommodate me with a single room, I asked the rate and then responded:

"We're getting the corporate rate here. If you can give us a similar discount, when I get back I'm going to educate our people about where to stay in Indianapolis."

This approach was no doubt enhanced by the fact that I made the call at about 10 P.M., when unoccupied rooms were going to remain that way. If the night manager refuses to accommodate you, when you are reserving your room in advance, try the assistant manager on the day shift. You may not get the corporate rate at every hotel with this approach but you will get it at good hotels in every price range in any major city in the country.

When you arrive, it's time for a little gentle upgrading at the reservations desk. You have the corporate rate but you know that all rooms at a given price are not equal. You may want something a little better than the hotel intended, or at least something that meets your specific preferences at no additional cost. You may want twin beds or a king- or queen-sized bed. You may be a light sleeper but the room assigned to you is on a fairly noisy floor because it faces street traffic or because other guests are inconsiderate. Maybe they're planning to put you over the outside incinerator vents, so that your sleep will be disturbed intermittently all night. If you're willing to accept random results, you may be checked into a room under the penthouse disco or near elevators that signal each approach to your floor with an audible "ping."

I prefer a quiet room with a view of the lake to being over the parking lot, with its predawn, cold-starting cars and revving motorcycles.

Make it clear when you check in that you'd like a quiet room with whatever is your preference in bed size. If you'd like to be on a particular side of the hotel, say so. You have every right to be a light sleeper and stating your needs in advance gives the hotel an opportunity to satisfy them. You are also building the record, preparing the groundwork that will facilitate resolution should something later go awry.

Before you see the room for the first time, you should have noted whether it's near the ice machine (a guaranteed disturbance of a night's sleep, often accompanied by loud conversations in slurred speech). Have the bellperson draw the curtains; look out and down. If you're not pleased, ask the bellperson to wait a moment. Call the reservations desk. State that you were promised a quiet room with a king-sized bed and explain in twenty-five words or less why this room isn't what you had in mind. Without waiting for an explanation, tell the desk that the bellhop is en route to pick up a key to a more suitable room and will meet you where you are to facilitate the room change.

When you hang up, tell the bellperson to make sure you get a room you'll like and that you'd appreciate it. Don't tip the bellperson yet. Surrender the key and smile. This is a minor, easily surmounted inconvenience that cannot disturb your equanimity. Up-scale people are not upset by this sort of trivia. They simply process it out of their lives. You don't want to be mistaken for an ordinary person who gets ordinary results. When you are in your new room, you will overtip the bellhop (What's an extra dollar or two in this context?) and later thank the desk by telephone. If something unforeseen makes the second room unsatisfactory, call the desk and explain why you need to be moved.

"They're sandblasting the gas company building across the street. I'm getting up early in the morning and have to get to sleep right away. I need a room on the other side of the hotel and I'd appreciate as much isolation as possible."

The star move, and one that marks you as a seasoned traveler, is to insist that a *four*-wheeled *cart* be sent up, *not* a *two*-wheeled hand truck, so that you may be moved conveniently, without repacking. Feel free to move in your pajamas and a robe. I've done so and have been relocated into suites at the ends of corridors surrounded only by peace and quiet, accompanied by a hotel bellhop and cart. Piece of cake.

If you're pleased with your stay you will want to be able to make the same arrangement automatically the next time. You may even want the same room or its duplicate on another floor. See the hotel manager on the day shift. This person usually hears only complaints from guests. You are about to tell him or her how wonderful everything has been. If there were any minor problems, don't mention them in this discussion. You've been so pleased you want to make the same arrangement again. You need a card you may present at the desk or some means of identification you may use in making your reservation, entitling you to your regular discount.

The precedent is already set. You're the satisfied customer, the frequent user, the loyal guest they spend big advertising dollars trying to reach. Shouldn't be difficult. Don't accept the offhand suggestion to ask for this manager the next time and he/she will take care of everything. People change jobs, leave town, forget or are otherwise out to lunch when you need them if you leave things to chance. Get the card.

This piece of identification can be put to work for you, not only at the hotel that issued it, but at other hotels in the same city (and elsewhere) and, indeed, with establishments other than hotels. Say, for example, you originally preferred to stay at some other hotel in this city but were refused the corporate rate, or that you'd like to try a different hotel next time, maybe the best hotel in town, if you can get your regular discount.

Waltz over to the hotel of your choice. Don't wear your sandals and Bermudas. Get the feel of the place. Use the health club (your hotel can probably arrange this for you via the concierge), have lunch or go directly to the manager's office.

"Joe Chandler does a good job at the Chadwick but you folks have them beat eight ways to Sunday. I prefer *this* hotel and I know some of our other people will, too. We're getting the corporate rate at the Chadwick and if you can match or beat their discount, we'd like to do business with you." Show him/her your card.

You've now introduced a little friendly competition into the conversation. Why shouldn't this hotel manager want to increase his/her 70 percent occupancy rate? You look and sound presentable and you're already getting a discount from a direct competitor.

With two hotel discount cards in your pocket, you're feeling pretty good, especially if you were able to reverse an initial refusal by the second hotel. You're ready to try the same approach with a limousine service or a car rental agency. This time, put your discount card from the higher-priced hotel on the desk. If the hotel manager wouldn't give you such a card but did open an account with you entitling you to a discount, say so confidently.

"We're getting a 20 percent discount at the Livermore and we'd like to open an account with you if you can give us a corporate discount."

Mentioning the Livermore (the best hotel in town or one

of the best) will conjure the prospect of substantial future business and thus make it seem more worthwhile for you to have a discount.

There may be times when you can't arrange a discount (immediately) but want to do business with that company anyway. Maybe your expenses are being paid by somebody else or you have a strong preference to stay at a particular hotel. In such cases, get an upgrade. Pay the standard rate for the room but ask for a suite or at least a deluxe room on a high floor or in the towers; pay the standard rate but get a premium car. Get something. Get free parking at the hotel or free use of the tennis courts or of the health club. These items cost the seller little or nothing out of pocket. If your car occupies one of dozens of empty spaces in their garage there is no outlay for the hotel but you save real dollars and they make a substantial profit by renting to you at their regular (high) price.

"All right. You win. We'll have somebody do all the paperwork. We'll do it your way this time and we'll pay the full civilian rate for the room if you can give us something special."

Don't overlook the weekend packages available at some hotels in big cities. Business travelers stay in hotels during the week while they conduct their business and leave in droves on weekends. This creates low weekend occupancy rates on a regular basis. Some hotels offer weekend packages in an effort to gain a competitive edge. The Convention and Tourist Bureau of the city you'll be visiting can provide details and availabilities in a single call or letter.

The typical weekend package involves two nights and gives you free parking, free health club and free breakfasts at about 40 percent less than the standard rate for the room alone. You will also find the facilities pleasantly uncrowded and have a good choice of rooms. The weekend package is an exceptional bargain, offering deluxe hotels at budget prices. If you are considering spending a weekend in a big city hotel that isn't offering a weekend package, tell the assistant manager (or somebody else who has the authority to make a deal) about the package a comparable hotel is offering.

"How can a loyal customer who is a frequent business traveler get a competitive arrangement at your hotel?"

You may be overlooking a number of other discounts. The company that employs you can probably arrange for you to have various credit cards in your name with their corporate discounts. If you have your own company, many corporate discounts are available to you without an annual dollar or volume commitment. Some car rental companies, for example, will give you about one third off their already low rates without any commitment. So-called senior citizen discounts are available on a variety of goods and services, including several travel items. All the membership benefits, including these discounts, are yours when you join an organization like the American Association of Retired Persons (located in Washington, D.C.). You don't have to be over sixty-five to join. Eligibility begins at age fifty-five and members need not be retirees either. In addition, *The Discount Guide for Travelers Over 55* by Caroline Wentz and Walter Wentz (New York: E. P. Dutton) provides a detailed breakdown of availabilities here and abroad.

Airlines also offer a number of special fares. Standby, advance purchase, promotional, charter, economy, business, first-class and other arrangements may be made. To complicate the market even further, there are triangular flights (you fly from A to B to C, with stopovers, then return to A), circle flights (you begin and end your flight in the same city with a number of stopovers en route) and open-jaw flights (you fly from A to B, proceed to C by some other means not on this ticket, and fly from C to A). There are also prime and fringe portions of the day, seasonal fluctuations and weekend discounts.

Until recently, in order to find the best available flights for your purpose, you had to do much comparison shopping, often relying on airline reservationists who were not sufficiently knowledgeable about their own company's offerings, or a travel agent who had a divided loyalty between you and the airline that paid his/her commissions. Beginning in 1984, however, and pioneered by Pan Am and TWA in this country, the entire reservation systems of airlines were made available to subscribers to national electronic information systems. Those with access to personal computers may now more easily discover the best deals, make their own reservations and even choose their own seats. Hotel and car rental agencies are almost certain to follow suit.

A good travel agent can make a difference, especially on pleasure trips and those that take you out of the country. Excellence among travel agents is at least as scarce as it is in other lines of work, however, and good results are further compromised by the divided loyalty mentioned earlier. The travel agent needs customers but is typically paid a commission by the seller of the travel service, not the customer.

A travel agent can often get you on flights and into hotels that are overbooked. Airlines and hotels overbook routinely because they know that many people who make reservations will fail to honor them without canceling. In order to boost load factors and occupancy rates, these sellers will try to overbook moderately, so that cancellations and no-shows will bring the totals of people to be accommodated under 100 percent of capacity. When anticipated cancellations and no-shows prove to be too high, some people with reservations are disappointed. As the travel agency is a high-volume customer, its clients can get a preference. Some corporations get a similar preference for the same reason.

The agent can also probably get you a discount or a package you were unaware of or were unable to get as an individual buyer. Other travel bargains, such as stopovers, special fares and closeouts (bargain rates for idle capacity on short notice) are also available through an agent. Some travel services sell memberships that provide two days at participating hotels for the price of one, or seven for five, standby or closeout flight availabilities and special travel packages. Most unions offer their members an array of travel bargains. If you don't buy a membership in one of these services and are not a union member (or member of some other group or profession so favored) you may nevertheless sometimes obtain the same arrangement by calling sellers who offer these deals and speaking with somebody who has the authority to give them to you.

"We'd love to spend a few days at Mondo Dolce. May we get the same deal as our friends who are members of the Director's Guild?" Or, "We'd love to try your restaurant but we don't have the discount book this year. Can you accommodate us?"

If you and your friends are going to a resort hotel, you may be able to arrange a quantity discount for yourselves by having one of you make all the reservations. A usual result would include a discount on the price plus a package of bonus items, such as free breakfasts, free greens fees and tennis charges, a basket of fruit and a bottle of champagne in the rooms, and the like. If you wish, you may then ask a travel agent to do better for you than you were able to do for yourselves.

A good travel agent also provides another avenue for recourse if something goes wrong. You will probably do better to deal with a member of the American Society of Travel

Agents (ASTA), as this assures a minimum of experience, plus bonding. Even better, some agents are also members of the Institute of Certified Travel Agents (ICTA).

Tour directors who are members of the United States Tour Operator's Association are also bonded. If you buy a foreign tour package, be sure to know exactly what's included, what's not included and what recourse you have, if any, if you don't get what you paid for. The only thing you may safely take for granted is that if an item is not specifically included, you will pay an additional amount for it if you can get it at all.

Ask the agent what extra charges will be incurred, whether the price is subject to change, whether tiny fractions of a day are included as full days, what equipment you will fly, the schedule, how much additional a single room is, whether the tour is cancelable by the other side and whether you may cancel without incurring a penalty. If you see the words "not responsible" in your contract, spend a couple of dollars on insurance. Many good deals are obtainable in other countries only if arrangements are made before you arrive. Good guidebooks to the places you'll be visiting are useful, obtainable in many public libraries and are usually fairly inexpensive.

With all of the variables inherent in travel, it's prudent not only to anticipate "the unexpected," but to know how to deal with it effectively. Hotel overbooking is a particularly irksome problem. Such overbooking, as was mentioned earlier, is often a function of the hotel's trying to protect itself against no-shows, and this might be pardonable if the hotel were not also stealing your money and downgrading your trip in many cases.

The standard hotel overbooking rip-off works like this. The hotel staff is extremely sorry you've been inconvenienced and want to show their good faith by booking you into another hotel. You are told that you will be staying at an equivalent hotel or one perhaps a bit better, at no additional cost to you. The second hotel is, in fact, inferior but you don't know this as you've probably never stayed at either hotel.

The first hotel gives you vouchers to be presented to the second hotel on arrival in lieu of payment, after making a telephone call confirming your reservation. While the call is being made, somebody tells you how crowded it is in the area and how lucky you are to be getting these new accommodations. Far from home, tired, and hopeful that your vacation is being salvaged, you are properly grateful. The first hotel (which may or may not, in fact, be overbooked) bills your credit card company at its usual rates for your accommodations, is billed by, and subsequently pays, the second hotel (which charges a lower rate for inferior accommodations) and pockets the difference, making a profit on this scam for impairing your trip.

If you are traveling out of the country, ask your agent about overbooking complaints at the places you're planning to stay. Try to arrange a guaranteed reservation, now available through some credit card companies. Ask for written confirmations of reservations from the hotel and your travel agent. Before you leave, find out which are the comparable hotels in the area so you may be alerted to a possible rip-off if you are told on arrival your reservations are not available.

Finally, if you accept the overbooked hotel's help and check into the hotel it suggests, get an appropriate discount or package if you're not impressed with the new accommodations. Tell the first hotel you will pay the second hotel directly and cancel the credit card payment to the first hotel, eliminating their profit for overbooking. Make it clear that you will be taking this matter up with the local authorities as well as your own travel agent if they cannot accommodate you (failed memories about available rooms are sometimes revived under this pressure) and mention the words "consequential damages" in local argot or in some other way that is understandable to the hotel staff. Don't be loud, intense or disorderly in any way and smile at all times.

If you're not absolutely delighted with the new arrangements, call or wire your travel agent and make your displeasure known. Make no threats or accusations but mention consequential damages, upset, indignity and great emotional stress affecting everybody traveling with you. Request immediate relief and demand to be updated continually as to progress.

If you fly much, get the free booklet *Air Travelers' Fly Rights* from the Civil Aeronautics Board (CAB) in Washington, D.C. The general rule on overbooking, the most common problem with airlines, is that if you have a confirmed airline reservation on a domestic flight and are "bumped," you are entitled to an immediate written explanation of the terms, conditions and limitations of denied boarding compensation. The current terms (as specified by the CAB) require that, unless the overbooking was caused by the substitution of a smaller aircraft for operational or safety reasons and unless the airline is able to book you on another flight that has a scheduled arrival time within two hours (in this country) or four hours (for a flight originating in this country with an international destination) of your original scheduled arrival time, you will be offered compensation equal to the price of the flight, but not less than $25 nor more than $200. You don't have to accept this offer; you may refuse it and seek other redress.

In resolving disputes with sellers of travel services, I've found that "high palatability" fosters agreement. I try to make the terms of settlement attractive by finding items of value to me the seller can provide at little or no out-of-pocket expense of itself. As we've seen, it's much less costly for a hotel (with which you are in dispute) to give you a deluxe room or a suite with a four-poster bed in a quiet location (which it wasn't going to rent that night anyway) than it is to give you a couple of free meals, despite the fact that it charges less for the food than the price differential between an ordinary room and a choice suite. The food costs real, hard, out-of-pocket dollars, while the cost to the hotel of giving you the otherwise unoccupied suite is essentially the same as that of the unacceptable room.

An airline that inconveniences you should be willing to retain your goodwill by giving you several thousand bonus miles in its frequent-flyer program (if you're not already a member, you may join with this bonus), coupons for free headsets and drinks in coach or economy, and if you're skillful or persistent, a trial membership (three months or so is not excessive) in their "VIP club." I've received all of these items, as well as a full refund for a needlessly unpleasant flight.

Companies selling travel services find the "comp," or complimentary item, a highly palatable "make-good." It is not only inexpensive for the seller to cancel a bill that involves a small or nonexistent downside, but it also minimizes the possibility of consequential damages. Breach of contract lawsuits brought by hotel guests or airline passengers and other travelers may recover damages that go beyond the sums paid the seller to include additional amounts for inconvenience and upset plans.

Understandably, hotels and airlines and other such sellers want to avoid these damages and the bad publicity that usually accompanies them. The news media find such recoveries amusing and give them much coverage. The way to avoid these consequences is to mollify the customer by comping the bill. You can facilitate the comping process by building the record with names, photographs (if convenient) and good notes.

Comping may also be a convenient way to avoid account-ability to top management by lower-level executives. This bit of knowledge can produce magical results if and when you become the beleaguered traveler. The manager of a depart-ment of the hotel in which you're staying, or even the general manager of the hotel, is rarely part of top management of the corporation or conglomerate that owns the hotel. Top corpo-rate management is usually hundreds or thousands of miles away. The hotel executive on the premises with whom you are discussing your grievance would often prefer to sweep the problem under the rug by comping it than have it brought to top management's attention. Why let a problem ricochet in a way that might be personally disadvantageous? No need to play with live ammunition when it's so easily defused.

Therefore, when planning a trip it's a good idea to find out whether the hotels in which you'll be staying are parts of larger companies and jot down the names of the presidents and chairpersons. A stockbroker, public librarian or the chief operator or supervisor on the reservations switchboard can supply this information toll-free or at the cost of a local telephone call. In a pinch you can often get instant relief by dropping one of these names into the conversation.

As more fully described in another book, my wife and I checked into a resort hotel in the Caribbean. After a couple of days, we couldn't take it any more and decided to make other reservations. Before checking out, I put some notes on a yellow legal pad, went to see the manager and aired a long list of grievances. At the conclusion of this recitation I won-dered aloud whether Mr. ———, the lofty chief executive of the conglomerate that owned the hotel, had any idea how the hotel was being run.

The manager, who had been allowing me to ventilate before getting on with his day, and who'd sat there impassively without making any offer at reparations, suddenly became animated. He insisted on comping the bill "as a personal favor to him." I had no trouble accommodating him and my wife and I proceeded to the next hotel.

Comping has become a push button so loosened with use that it falls into place easily, especially when combined with the slightest implication of jeopardy for its dispenser. This jeopardy is so feared, it is sometimes inferred even when unintended. During a book publicity tour, I stayed in the towers of a hotel that is part of a large chain and was given two tickets (one for each night's stay) for complimentary Continental breakfasts. The next morning I sauntered into the designated tower suite for the free breakfast and sat on a divan munching a Danish with my coffee and juice, intermittently watching David Hartman on a giant screen. A business-suited, white-haired gentleman finished his breakfast and headed for the elevators. His coterie of younger, similarly attired colleagues hastily gobbled their Danishes and swigged their coffee, or threw their napkins atop what remained of their meagre breakfasts. They scrambled in his wake like chicks fearful of abandonment by a mother hen, lest they miss his elevator car.

The following morning I dialed room service and told the person who answered the telephone that I was going to have a big breakfast. As there was an opportunity to save my publisher a few dollars, I asked to have the juice, toast and coffee at no charge in exchange for the ticket entitling me to a complimentary Continental breakfast. Told this was impossible, I requested the room service manager. After we exchanged names, I repeated the request and got the same response.

"Impossible, Mr. ———? I'm watching a launching of the space shuttle on television as we speak, which is a lot more difficult feat, it seems to me, than your simply omitting a couple of items from my breakfast check in exchange for this ticket. One of my friends was Barron Hilton's college roommate and I would imagine Mr. Hilton would be astonished to learn you thought this routine request was impossible."

When the cart arrived, I was told the entire breakfast was "compliments of the hotel," which wasn't the point but I accepted it.

You can create a surprisingly valuable package of travel benefits for yourself by combining better planning, a more complete understanding of the marketplace and some fairly elementary negotiating techniques. As a business traveler you should be able to enjoy lower rates and preferred treatment. If, on occasion, you are displeased, you are the frequent traveler, the high-volume user, the preferred customer who will be given special treatment.

When you are traveling for pleasure, especially if you will be out of the country, a good, carefully selected travel agent should be working to make your trip enjoyable and uncomplicated. This agent can also be used as a buffer as well as another corrective lever should something untoward develop. As the agent does much other business with the hotels and other establishments with which you'll be dealing, this fact of business life should work to your advantage in smoothing the rough spots.

In a rare case that cannot be corrected on the site, the agent may also provide a level of legal recourse and this possibility may help to enlist the agent's best efforts to make you whole. With these screens in place to protect your business and pleasure trips, you should be immune to most of the problems and disappointments that arise. The small residue, too, will likely yield with a little practice and confidence in communicating what you need and want to make your travels enjoyable.

One more suggestion. The National Safety Council (444 North Michigan Avenue, Chicago, Illinois 60611; (312) 527-4800) has published a valuable flyer entitled "How to Survive a Hotel Fire." It is available to nonmembers at 20 cents per copy in a minimum order of 50, plus $3.00 for postage and handling, for a total of $13 (Stock No. 195.83). The same information is also available in a wallet card (Stock No. 195.85) on the same basis, or it may be obtained in the form of a luggage tag ($2.80 each, no minimum order). Prices, as always, are subject to change.

☐ Stockbrokers

In the securities business, the customer's brokers who earn the most money are the ones who make the most money for the companies that employ them, not for the customers whose accounts they service. They are customarily paid, directly or indirectly, on the basis of the gross commissions they generate, not on performance, ability, skill, honesty, competence or the willingness to correct their own, or the company's, errors and omissions. Your customer's broker has a vested interest in getting you to trade and is flogged to do so in one sales meeting after another, yet he/she knows (or should know) that the more you trade, the less likely you are to profit. Unless you appreciate this fundamental conflict of interest between you and your customer's broker, you are playing for a draw down the exchange and two pawns.

The second basic point on this subject is that your customer's broker can cost you much more than commissions, interest and fees. With a few standard ploys and only slightly more than the average lack of scrupulousness in the industry, your customer's broker can nudge you, by degrees, into the fast lane to Tap City. There are endless variations with more to come, no doubt, but here are some of the more blatant monetary muggings to be avoided.

THE HOT TIP

At a point chosen by your customer's broker you are confidentially informed that said broker has a friend downtown with a particularly acute ear who is privy to extremely important financial inside information. You are invited to participate in the profits certain to flow from such privileged information, profits which have already flowed so copiously for other selected clients with whom said customer's broker has been generously sharing said information. You are told that speedy action on the information is necessary as it is usually made public in a matter of hours after your broker's friend informs your broker.

You are thrilled and delighted to be availed this extraordinary opportunity and pledge speed and confidentiality. If you need a little convincing of said friend's auditory acuity, it will soon be supplied. The broker will impart some inside information from this source within a fortnight. You will be given the terms of a stock split or merger or other important piece of financial news for demonstration purposes only. A couple of hours later, your broker will call you and announce that the inside information you received earlier is coming across the Dow Jones news ticker at that very moment, precisely as foretold. You are impressed, convinced and properly grateful.

There is, of course, no friend downtown and no inside information. Your broker chooses important items he/she sees being printed on the Dow Jones news ticker and feeds this public news to you as "inside information." Later in the day, the broker will call to report that the previously imparted "inside information" is then being made public, confirming his/her "important source."

This scam has two principal variations. In variation one, the broker is generating commissions in a dishonest, criminal manner by gaining your confidence in this infallible source. You may actually take an occasional profit on such a trade, but more often than not you will lose money as you will be coming into the game on stale news. In any case, you are being fleeced for commissions which may well be augmented by the fact that you have to sell something you already own in order to participate in the "inside information."

Variation two is even more sinister. Your broker hears a single bell sounded by the Dow Jones news ticker, heralding an important news item. He/she gazes intently at the ticker on the front wall of the brokerage office or pockets an order form and scampers to the side of the room, where a paper or acetate ticker prints the identical news. This ticker's print-out is available a few seconds earlier than that projected on the office wall as the latter must first travel through the projector.

Say, for example, the particular item being printed leads with this headline: "XYZ PLANS 3 FOR 1 STOCK SPLIT, RAISES DIVIDEND." The customer's broker whirls into action. He/-she (rightly or wrongly) interprets this news as bullish for XYZ stock and writes out an order to buy X hundred shares of XYZ at the market. The broker then dashes to the order desk and enters the order.

The order form has spaces for the account number and the name of the account. Proper procedure requires that both a name and a number appear on the order at the time it is entered. If supervision is lax enough in this office to permit neither a name nor a number to be affixed to an entered order, this scam is facilitated. However, to take the some-what more difficult case for the broker, assume that both a name and an account number are required and have been supplied in this case. The larcenous broker circumvents the procedure by deliberately mismatching the name and the number.

The broker then returns to his/her desk and awaits developments. Several clients have been impressed by this broker's access to "inside information" and have expressed their eagerness to participate in it even if they are telephonically inaccessible when such information becomes available to the broker. The broker is instructed to use his/her discretion in such cases and to place an order accordingly, perhaps limited by the customer as to the size of the order.

The larcenous broker has placed the name of one of these discretionary accounts on the order to buy XYZ stock. The number on the order, however, is that of the broker or his/her nominee. If the stock rises sufficiently, the profit will be the broker's, either directly or via the nominee and he/she will conform the name on the order to the number, or simply do nothing, aware that the number will control the trade. If the stock declines, the loss will be the customer's and the thieving broker will change the number on the order to conform to the name during the trading session, after sufficient time has elapsed to foreclose an opportunity for profit. The broker, of course, will have generated commissions in any case. If the trade shows a loss, all that may remain is the "re-close," a little sales pitch to assuage buyer remorse with a losing trade. The lyric is simple and the music is given an up-tempo beat in order to transform a dirge into a serenade:

Broker: My friend downtown called again today and told me XYZ was going to split three for one and raise the dividend. You were the first person I called but I couldn't reach you. (This vague reference covers all the bases, for it includes those times the customer was not in as well as those when his/her line(s) were busy, and of course no time has been given for the attempted call.)

Well, I knew you'd want in on information like this, so I bought you two hundred. And what do you think? A little while ago, the company announces a three for one split and they raised the dividend. My friend was right again. How about that guy!

Customer: Thanks a lot, Phil. That's great. How much did I pay?

Broker: 84½.

Customer: How much is it now?

Broker: It's off a small fraction (actually, the stock is selling at 82⅞ and beginning to stabilize; the customer has a loss of $325 plus commissions as they speak) but what's the difference? You know, Charlie, not every broker on the street has a source like this. It may take a little while but this one should work out all right.

The chances of your receiving profitable inside information from your customer's broker are approximately zero, and if you do receive such information, there are laws against its dissemination that may embarrass you. You may easily check your broker's source of this sort of "inside information" by visiting a brokerage office before the close on the day you receive it, locating the paper (or acetate) news copy, finding the news item and noting the time it was printed, which appears at the end of the item. You may then compare this time with that when your broker reached you with the news from "his friend downtown."

In those cases when you were "not available" to your broker's "call," visit your broker's office the same day he/she bought stock in your account based on "inside information," ask to see the executed order (the one the order clerk entered, a copy of which was returned to your broker) and compare the time it was entered (the earlier time on the order) with the time the Dow Jones news service printed the item. Subtract a little time for the time it took to complete the body copy after the headline was printed. If your order was not entered prior to this time, your broker has some explaining to do.

If your broker is so eager to get you through life's financial mazes, make it clear that you prefer he/she do that by reserving 25 or 50 shares out of his/her allotment of a few hot issues each year. The best advice, however, is not to deal with a dishonest broker, if only because it is a matter of time before the broker's dishonesty costs you money. In any case, judge your broker on the basis of performance. When investing or trading, the bottom line is the bottom line.

THE MISQUOTATION

This one is so rampant it is even suggested at sales meetings. The customer is first described by the sales manager, or the equivalent company executive, as a "chiseler." The customer's brokers in attendance who have not yet fallen asleep chuckle their acquiescence.

"If you haven't already educated your clients to buy and sell 'at the market' (to buy at the offered price and sell on the bid), you're making a big mistake. First of all, it's a nuisance to write out an order to buy a stock a quarter or a half a point under the last sale, or a sell order a small fraction above the last sale."

The sales manager holds up a stack of unexecuted orders:

"Look at this waste! These are last week's unexecuted orders in this office! They represent wasted time, effort and *money* for all of us. Now, let me show you how to convert this waste into *what,* Chester? Will somebody wake him up! We're talking about converting this waste into *commissions!*"

The instructions for this conversion are simple. When a customer asks for a quote on a stock, the broker almost invariably knows whether the customer is thinking of buying or selling it. The broker knows the customer and his/her trading patterns. The broker knows whether the customer already owns the stock in most cases, and if so, at a profit or a loss. If there is the slightest doubt, the broker may simply ask (during the time it takes to get the customer's quote), "What do you hear?" The customer will then indicate by the response whether the intent is a purchase or a sale of the stock.

With that information in hand, the waste conversion process moves forward. Say the actual quote on the stock is 81–81½. The highest bid at the moment is $81 per share, the lowest offered price is $81.50. If the customer is a buyer, the broker knows he/she might enter an order to buy at 81¼ or at a lower price. If the stock firms during the day, the order won't be executed at the price it was entered and the customer may decide not to chase the stock. Even if the stock were to sell off slightly toward the close, the customer may change his/her mind before that happens and cancel the order. In these cases, there will be no trade, no commission, ergo "waste."

In order to deal with this "chiseler," the broker simply lies. If the broker knows the client is a buyer, the quote is raised a fraction; in this case, to, say, 81¼–81¾. If the customer wants to sell, he/she receives a low quote, of perhaps 80¾–81¼, or some such distortion. If the customer then bids 81½ or offers stock at 81 on this misinformation, he or she is actually selling on the bid or buying at the offered price. The order will almost certainly be executed (hence no dreaded waste). Whether the particular trade leads to a profit or a loss is not the point. In every case, the dishonest broker is playing with a deck stacked against the customer, in every case the trade means a commission for the house and the customer's broker and in many of these trades the customer is being nicked with fractional losses each time he/she buys and sells. In addition, this sort of dishonesty tends to feed on itself; the dishonest broker will likely find other ways to inflict additional losses on the customer.

The way to uncover this problem is to test your broker from time to time. Pick an active and volatile stock you don't own that's selling for more than $70 per share. This is an excellent candidate for the kind of dishonesty this test is designed to reveal.

Get a quote on the stock from a disinterested discount broker or from a quote machine. Immediately call your broker and ask for a quote on the same stock. Your broker will assume you are considering its purchase. If asked, don't dispel this illusion. "I like the stock," is all you need reply. If your broker quotes the offered price as higher than the price you were quoted seconds earlier, immediately recheck the quote with another source.

For best results, make the call from another brokerage office with a quote machine near at hand. If the quoted offered price is lower than that supplied by your broker, repeat the test in a week or two. If your broker fails both tests, assuming you performed the tests rigorously (by keeping the time lags between quotes to a matter of seconds or, better, eliminating them entirely by having the stock on the screen while you called your broker), you've got a problem.

THE NOT-SO-SPECIAL "SPECIAL" SITUATION

From time to time, a large holder of a stock wants to sell his/her position without disturbing the market with a huge supply. There are a number of reasons for such large sales but say, for example, the president or chairperson of a publicly traded company dies with a million shares of the company's stock and the legatees or executors decide to sell it. The market in the stock cannot absorb a million shares without tumbling. Therefore, what is often done is to consult a brokerage house for the purpose of arranging to offer the stock *away* from the market via a secondary distribution. The brokerage house, usually in concert with other such houses, arranges to sell the million shares at a negotiated price (close to the current price) for a handsome fee.

In order to induce customers' brokers to sell this stock to their clients, the customers' brokers are offered an unusually high commission in the form of a "discount." This payment is typically almost double the usual commission for a similarly priced stock. The inducement to the customer is that the stock is offered on "a net basis"; that is, the customer pays no commission.

This sale of stock is a secondary (as opposed to a primary) offering. In the case of a primary offering, the company sells stock never previously held by the public and the company gets the proceeds of the sale. Thus, while there is a large, new supply of stock created, it is balanced by the fact that the company receives cash for it and is presumably that much stronger by virtue of the cash infusion.

In a secondary offering, however, such as the one discussed here, the company will not get any money. The proceeds of the sale will go to the seller's estate, not to the company. Thus, a large supply of stock will be passing from one pair of strong hands (those of the late president or chairperson) to many pairs of weak hands (those of the public), with no counterbalancing gain to the company.

When a large potential supply of stock overhangs any market with no compensating factors, the tendency is for the stock involved to decline in price. In order to disguise the important distinction between a primary offering (by a company, in which the latter will get the proceeds of the sale) and a secondary offering like the one described here, your broker (probably coached by his/her sales manager) refers to both types as "special offerings," blurring this distinction. Thus, your broker is not telling you the whole truth and, at the same time, is in a complete conflict of interest with you in recommending your participation in this secondary.

In order to make an informed choice, ask your broker whether the offering is a primary or a secondary distribution and who is getting the proceeds of the sale. Then ask for confirmation of this by mail. If it is not forthcoming, you should act accordingly. There are too many other ways to make money to be concerned about riding a secondary to a profit.

(UN)TRUE ROMANCES

Your broker calls you with a romantic story about a stock and recommends that you buy it. You've never heard of the stock but the story is designed to whet your appetite for profit. As in the case of "the hot tip," in addition to the commission for the broker on this purchase, there's a fair chance you may need to sell something in order to buy the romantic stock, thus creating two commissions. In this case, there may be an additional factor at work. Your broker may be acting as a dealer.

Most brokerage firms act as brokers on some trades and as dealers on others. As a broker, the function is that of an agent who goes into the market and buys or sells on your instructions. As a dealer, the function is that of a principal who buys stock from you or sells to you for the firm's own account. In this latter capacity of dealer, it is as if your real estate agent were selling you his/her own property or buying yours. Even a naive client should want to know why somebody who knows much more about the stock than the client, so much more in fact that they are dealers in it, is so eager to sell it if it's so sure to go higher.

One clue to the fact that your broker is acting as a dealer is that there will be (or should be) no commission on the trade. Your customer's broker will probably point this out to you as an inducement. What this person may not tell you is that you will probably be buying the stock on the offered price. If the stock is quoted 20–20½ (a wide spread on a $20 stock and one the brokerage house controls, as it is a dealer in the stock and is making this market), you'll probably pay 20½ net, allowing ample room in the trade for your customer's broker to be paid a commission (often called a "credit" in these cases) and for the firm to take a profit. More important, the firm is also unloading some unwanted inventory on guess who.

The second clue is (or should be) on the confirmation slip. There is coded information on the slip that specifies the marketplace in which the trade was executed and whether the firm acted as a broker (agent) or a dealer (principal). Before you succumb to one of these true romances, ask your customer's broker whether the firm is acting as a broker or a dealer. If the latter, you're on your own. As in the case of secondary offerings, not every such trade will produce a loss; only most (especially if you factor in the return on the funds otherwise utilized or put at interest). If you have the slightest doubt about the trade, the prudent course is to pass. You may miss an occasional opportunity for profit but you'll be miles ahead in the long run.

If you're shopping for a customer's broker, it's a good idea to find a brokerage house and a specific office of that firm that suits you, then choose the specific customer's broker. There are a number of good reasons for this but the major one is the way broker error is handled. Some brokerage houses are straightforward about acknowledging their own errors, taking responsibility for them and correcting them at once. Others will deny them, go to great lengths to cover them up, stonewall the customer and even deliberately mislead exchange and agency investigators in efforts to evade liability. With the high volume of trading in current markets there is no shortage of broker errors. If you do business with a house that is not conscientious about correcting their own mistakes, it's only a matter of time before a costly broker error finds its way to your account. Take some pains to prevent this source of financial loss by choosing a firm carefully. Should you become aware of uncorrected broker error, close the account to prevent any recurrence and enlist the aid of management, the exchange and the Securities and Exchange Commission to have the error corrected.

To help you find a reliable house and office, ask a number of successful business and professional people you respect whether they're happy with their brokerage firm. Eliminate the street-level offices. These tend to attract the public and take on some of the atmosphere of a gambling casino. Crowd psychology can limit your performance. Customer's brokers (too close to the minutiae of the market anyway, so that insignificant data tend to become exaggerated) are easily swept up by the crowds in street-level brokerage offices. Look at the members of these crowds carefully. Do they look more like people living off interest and dividends or candidates for Gamblers Anonymous?

It's also a plus if your broker doesn't smoke and isn't alcoholic or obese. I take these to be signs of too much emotional involvement with the market (or even more serious problems) to permit careful judgment and relaxed moneymaking. It's my experience that you can't fight the market or press too hard and take consistent profits. That's one of the reasons it's a good idea to be out of the market some of the time. Your broker, unfortunately, is in the pressure cooker fifty or fifty-two weeks per year, often eating lunch at the desk as well. I prefer to shun signs of pressure in this context and street-level offices and these personal indicia of them are best avoided.

Visit the firms recommended to you and get the feel of them. Ask customers how broker error is treated. The customer's broker I'm looking for should be honest, experienced and competent, with an absence of too much greed or need, so that I get my share of the goodies with none of the garbage. I would therefore prefer to open an account with somebody in the office who has a title (office manager, assistant manager, department manager), somebody who has been on the job for several years and somebody who looks and acts like a winner. People with titles usually have more clout and more staying power, both in the firm and in the industry, so you won't have to repeat the search process from scratch as often. After you're satisfied that you're in a good office, ask the office manager to help you select the right customer's broker but be sure to avoid the "broker of the day."

The broker of the day is the customer's broker to whom all "walk-ins" and "call-ins" are routinely referred on a given day. Say, for example, you visit a brokerage office and want to get some information or open an account. You will be referred to customer's broker A. The following day, it will be customer's broker B's turn. As some of these encounters lead to the opening of new accounts and accounts generate commissions, the customer's brokers are willing to go along with the inconveniences on the chance that a little wheat may be found among the chaff. Some are even more than willing—they are insistent. For this reason, the office manager who spends five minutes listening to your list of qualifications for a prospective customer's broker will probably nod knowingly and tell you he/she has exactly the person for you, then refer you to broker A if this is the broker of the day and to broker F if you come back five business days later.

As forced choices like this are not designed to deliver best results, take the precaution of calling the office before your visit. Tell the switchboard operator you're thinking of opening an account. When you're referred to Mr./Ms. A, this is presumably the broker of the day. All you need then do is make sure the manager doesn't "match" your needs with broker A. As a further precaution, when you arrive, ask a broker near the entrance who the broker of the day is. Then, if the manager attempts to foist this person on you, you are ready:

"I have no quarrel with the broker of the day but the handling of my accounts is much too important a matter to be left to chance."

You may find you need more than one customer's broker even if you don't trade much or have a large portfolio. A discount broker may save you money on commissions but a so-called full-service broker may make a number of free services available to you and also charge a lower interest rate on your debit balance. You can arrange to get the best of both worlds and even to improve each of the worlds by having accounts at more than one broker, and exerting some competitive pressure.

You may not have to deal with more than one broker in order to make the broker who services your account more responsive. Say, for example, you're dealing with a full-service firm. You value their research facilities, the use of their library, good advice, good executions, the fact that their telephone lines are not jammed during peak hours, your occasional invitation to participate in hot new issues and other advantages and are therefore willing to pay somewhat higher commissions than the low rates available at a no-frills discount broker. However, you know that some of the full-service broker's customers are paying lower commission rates than you and you realize that commissions are negotiable. How can you save a few hundred dollars annually?

First, get some good current information. Look at the advertisements in the financial press. *Barron's* carries ads featuring discount commission rates in every issue or you may make a few local or toll-free calls to discount brokers you see advertised elsewhere and get their rates. Compare these low rates with what your broker charges you. Call your broker or (better) visit him/her when he/she is not likely to be busy or surrounded by other clients, perhaps a few minutes after the close of the market. Take the advertised rates you found in the ads or were given over the telephone with you, as well as one or more confirmation slips executed for you by this broker.

Tell your broker you enjoy doing business with him/her but that you're paying $X per hundred shares of a $30 stock and many other brokers are charging considerably less. Show the broker an actual example from your own trading. Explain that broker A is charging only $Y for the same trade and broker B charges even less. Show your broker the actual numbers. Your broker knows these numbers are accurate. Pause here and wait for a response. This is a familiar subject. The firm has undoubtedly furnished your broker with a standard response.

"You won't get the kind of services we provide at a discount broker. Nobody will monitor your stocks and keep you informed about them. We have many more floor clerks and floor brokers so you get better executions. We also have the best research department in the industry. All of this costs a lot of money and yours is only a small account. We don't make much money on small accounts. That's why the firm has a policy on discounts that's based on the size of the account. You know, it costs as much for us to execute a trade on a 100-share order as it does on a 1,000- or 5,000-share order so small accounts pay a little more but they get a lot more."

Listen to the explanation without argument or interruption. Don't be offended by any of the defensive rhetoric. When it's again your turn to speak, reply that you appreciate what was said by way of response, that many good points were made, that you like to deal with the firm and enjoy the relationship with the broker.

"I'm a low-overhead account. My orders are always close to the market. You don't have to spend much time servicing my account. I also pick my own stocks so I don't profit from the research department. I'm not asking for a 50 percent discount but I think I'm entitled to pay less than the absolute maximum the firm charges. Many customers get discounts."

If this doesn't find ready agreement, listen to the explanation.

"I want to have a good, long-term relationship with you and the firm. I'm not asking for the moon. If you can't help me, who in the firm can?"

Your request to mitigate the firm's commission rates in

your account almost undoubtedly does not go beyond your broker's authority, especially if your broker is somebody with a title, which was an earlier suggested preference in a broker. A small discount should present no problem for most customer's brokers, and certainly not for any manager or assistant manager. At a minimum, you should be able to get at least a 20 percent discount off the top rate.

After the broker has agreed to an acceptable discount and you've been assured the new rate will be implemented at once, acknowledge your broker's cooperation. You appreciate this narrowing of the commission gap and you look forward to further moderation when your volume of trading or debit balance rises enough to warrant it. Speaking of debit balances, however, you have one more request and this won't cost your customer's broker a penny but will help you. Would he or she be good enough to have the firm lower the exorbitant interest rate you've been paying on your margin debt?

In truth, this takes nothing from your customer's broker. His or her income is not affected. Again, your customer's broker can probably take at least 1 percent off the top rate you've probably been paying (especially if yours is a small account) and this can be a significant annual saving for you if you have even a modest five-figure debit balance. Brokers usually charge their customers between ½ percent and 2½ percent above the prime rate, compounded monthly, so there is ample room in which to bargain. A 1 percent reduction from the high end of this range is a good first objective, with the expectation of lowering the interest rate (and commission rates) further if the amount you owe or your volume of trading increases significantly. Don't be stymied by the standard response that the firm charges *all* accounts with debit balances under a certain amount (that includes yours) the highest rate, with a sliding scale of lower rates as the debt mounts. Remind your broker that rates are negotiable, that others are paying less and that you'd prefer equal treatment with those paying *less,* not more.

There are some additional items of value your broker can provide. Don't ask for them in this meeting but get your share. Stock charts, access to the financial library, occasional copies of monthly stock guides and even some shares of a hot, new issue (the ones that open at handsome premiums) come readily to mind as a way to close the commission gap. Somebody is getting this lagniappe. All you want is your share, which is more than nothing.

It may sometimes be necessary to open an account with another broker and to point out to each the particular advantage you enjoy with the other. Broker A, whose firm charges lower commissions, would be told of broker B's lower interest rates or generosity with hot issues, and vice versa. This is designed to stimulate both brokers to give you a better mix of rates and services, and the competitive pressure may help each win a point for you with management, if necessary.

Scrutinize the forms your broker presents for signature before you sign them. If you are handed any forms in person, tell your customer's broker you'll mail them back and put them out of sight while you are with the broker. If you don't happen to have something convenient in which to carry them, ask the broker for an envelope. Don't make the mistake of signing these documents at once and handing them back to your broker. They are contracts that were drawn by the seller's lawyers and they have been continually updated as statutory and case law dictate. They are drawn to protect the seller's interests and contain state-of-the-art pitfalls and traps for the unwary customer. These documents routinely strip buyers of fundamental rights.

Some customer agreements, for example, expressly eliminate the broker's legal liability for "ordinary" negligence, exposing the broker only in those rare, almost nonexistent cases in which you can prove "gross," "willful" or "wanton" negligence. Thus, by defining negligence, a substandard and inadequate level of performance that has been actionable in Anglo-Saxon jurisprudence for centuries, and properly so, as "ordinary," the effect is to raise a wholly unacceptable, careless and damaging way of doing business to legitimacy in a wondrous bit of legerdemain accomplished in no more time than it takes to sign your name. Agreements, by their nature, are not ultimatums. They are subject to negotiation and modification. There are many ways to implement desired changes in these customer agreements. Perhaps the simplest is to rule straight lines through unacceptable language in indelible ink, then sign and return the document. I've done this with brokers on more than one occasion and the deletions were never questioned or called to my attention, suggesting a bit of "ordinary" negligence on the part of the back-office staffs.

You won't be aware of most of the costly errors and omissions that affect your stock brokerage accounts. If needless delay on the part of your customer's broker or anybody else (order clerk, floor clerk, floor broker) involved in getting your order to its destination causes you to miss the market, for example, the chances of your finding it out are close to zero. In those rare cases when you do detect a costly broker error or negligent act, the firm should be willing to make it good at once. You should also observe how your customer's broker handles orders. If he/she doesn't give top priority to entering good orders, get another broker.

Above all, be guided by performance. The securities markets are not the only places to put your money to work. Some people who are successful in other moneymaking activities do not do well in stocks or bonds. The intelligent course, if this applies to you, is not to fight the market. If your first few attempts show a net loss, or if after a year or two you don't show a reasonable net return, I would urge you to find another medium for your money that is more compatible for you.

In any event, the best general advice I can offer in this context is this: don't permit a big loss. You must have the discipline to limit losses. Occasional small losses of perhaps as much as 10 or 15 percent cannot do a great deal of damage but big losses can wipe out your capital. If you find yourself taking big losses, I would suggest you get out of the market and stay out. This is a sure sign that you're in the wrong game. The hardest wounds to heal are the self-inflicted ones. You deserve better treatment at your own hands.

The only other investment advice I would offer is to let your profits run. The decision to take a profit is more complicated but I would suggest the following as a kind of rule of thumb that will prevent a big loss and permit big profits. When you take a position, decide on what will be your maximum loss, say 10 to 15 percent from where you got in. Place an open stop order at that point. If the trade goes this much against you, it will be reversed into cash with this level of loss.

If, however, the trade goes in your favor, keep changing the price of your open stop order in the direction of your profit so that the price remains about 15 percent off the closing price that showed the maximum profit to date for your trade. There may be a rare occasion when you are extremely close to a long-term gain and would be willing to risk a moderately smaller profit in order to turn a short-term gain into a long-term one. In such a rare case, you may decide to cancel your stop order until the trade goes long-term, at which time you will reinstate it and keep changing it as suggested. This kind of disciplined approach permits you to take substantial profits without ever incurring a big loss instead of the reverse, which, alas, is all too often the case.

☐ Home
Improvements

This one is a real briar patch, a major source of consumer complaints all over the country. Billions of dollars are energetically siphoned each year from homeowners bent on improving their lot. This massive quid pro nil is carried out by an industrious army of career scamsters, licensed incompetents, journeymen dispensers of shoddy, substandard, overpriced work, and their apprentices, busily mastering the art of succeeding in business without actually trying. Do the numerous fleecings administered by these gifted shepherds imply that you, too, may soon be misled by some crook? Is it only a matter of time before you are taken to the cleaners one fine spring? By no means. Even if you don't know a grout from a titmouse you are home free if you but follow a few simple principles.

First, make it an inviolable rule that you will seek those whom you want to hire on each and every home improvement project you undertake, not vice versa. As virtually all home improvement scams begin with somebody knocking at your door, calling you on the telephone, writing you a letter or placing an advertisement in a newspaper, if you actively choose your own cast of home improvement characters, you will automatically finesse 99 and $^{44}/_{100}$ percent of the career scamsters. Strict adherence to this simple first principle is not an unmixed blessing, for you will miss a number of scamster-inspired dramatic moments without which life may sometimes seem dull. You will never get to know any of the "inspectors" who discover termites undermining the structure of your house, or your dangerously faulty furnace or some badly worn electrical wiring certain to burn your house down while the family is asleep. You won't receive the benefit of their sober recommendations of emergency repair people to do the work immediately, competently and at the right price, nor will you be able to thank them for accepting your good faith in calling the recommended professionals as sufficient reason not to report any of the dangerous conditions you were harboring to the authorities or give you a citation.

You will also forgo the opportunity to share a soft drink with the public-spirited chimney repairer who noticed some loose bricks in your chimney in time to prevent impending tragedy from being visited upon some children playing under it. You will also, alas, not chance to meet any of the itinerant driveway and roof repairers who happen to have some materials left over from a job recently completed in the neighborhood and could do a similar job for you at a bargain price. Nor will you be able to watch their substandard, over-priced materials wash off your roof and stain the side of your house the next time it rains or simply ooze down your drive and, along with your money, disappear into the drain. You will also miss the opportunity presented to a confederate of one or more of these vagabond scamsters to steal some valuables from your house in broad daylight, on one pretext or another, while the scamster at or near your front door occupies your attention with his oft-repeated sales pitch.

There are dozens of imaginative variations on these scams and new and more efficient methods for hoodwinking homeowners are in continual research and development. However, despite much overtime work and the assistance of cadres of sprightly new recruits, the demand for these services continues to outstrip the supply. Strict adherence to this first principle will deliver you from these scams but it won't automatically guarantee your satisfaction with the home improvements you buy. For this, you will need more. For presentation purposes, I'll use the example of a major renovation, restoration, rehabilitation or remodeling project, a complicated undertaking involving several professions, crafts, trades and specialties, a fair amount of time and a serious amount of money, precisely the kind of job for which Grecian Formula was invented. If you can get this project done to your complete satisfaction, every other home improvement job you contemplate should be Betty Crocker time.

Some homeowners punish themselves unnecessarily during the course of a renovation. Painfully aware of the high costs and the many frustrations, these self-flagellants then compare themselves unfavorably with their ancestors, who were able to fashion a place to live out of an unfriendly wilderness with an ax and a few simple tools. There is nothing to feel guilty or unworthy about nor any need for those so afflicted to punish themselves by hiring the wrong help and running up the costs and frustrations even further. Those ancestors who built their own houses four or five generations ago didn't have heat or hot water, electricity, air-conditioning, in-ground swimming pools, tennis courts, lanais or even driveways, nor were they particularly concerned about resale values. They weren't required by law to be licensed in any craft or profession. They didn't need permits, weren't subject to inspections, zoning laws or building codes, all of which might have stymied a Leonardo and surely would have kept him from doing more important work.

A useful image to keep in mind during a renovation is to think of yourself as a Broadway producer. You have this naggingly great idea for a play but it's a bit vague, it's going to require the help of several other people working collaboratively, it costs money and time and it entails risks. What's the crucial element I left out? If you said a script, I owe you a gold star. This leads to the second principle, a basic axiom from the theater: if it ain't on the page, it ain't on the stage.

Once you get beyond cleaning, sanding, simple household repairs, touch-ups and some painting and polishing, any of which even ten-thumbed do-it-yourselfers can tackle behind the line of scrimmage on a sunny weekend, and enter the world of renovation, restoration, remodeling or rehabilitation, you need a plan. This written plan is your script, without which nothing. In the case of a play, if you need a script, you hire a playwright. In the case of a house, if you want a good plan tailored to your present and future needs, one that will also utilize the space more creatively and productively, provide esthetic satisfaction and be practical and feasible, you hire an architect.

A good architect is the best person to coordinate all the details of your project. He or she has the design sense and technical knowledge to translate your inchoate needs and desires into a house that works and looks good, too. If the work you plan involves structural changes or may alter the existing heating or cooling systems, plumbing or electricity in any major way, the need for an architect is even greater. Poorly planned work affecting any of these elements can seriously damage your house and your insurance may not cover the risks. A properly designed architectural plan, which may be incorporated into all future contracts that affect the house, eliminates all of these problems from the outset. The architect's plan will also take account of national and local codes and regulations. He or she can design a plan that includes your ideas and those of the others who will be living in the house. The cohesive and unified living space thus conceived is in sharp contrast to the uncoordinated and clumsy results that all too often flow from hiring a number of individuals to work their separate wills on the elephant from their own limited points of view in the absence of a comprehensive plan.

The architect eliminates all of this disharmony by designing an organic whole. The plan need not be executed at any one time. It may be subdivided to accommodate your finances and your schedule. Without such a plan, you can't reasonably expect to make major changes in your house and reach an equally satisfying result in design, quality or cost.

In hiring the right architect to help you get your project on its feet, it is well to invest your time before you invest your money. You will need recommendations. The general principle here is to seek recommendations from those who can make an informed suggestion and who have a genuine interest in your success with the project but no special interest in the person recommended. Avoid recommendations from sources that stand to profit if you take the offered advice. For example, it's easy to ask a lumber-mill owner or manager to recommend a carpenter but you are likely to hear only the names of carpenters who buy from that mill when the best carpenter in the area may not be a customer of that mill. If you seek long-term relationships with random results, you might as well simplify the task and use the classified telephone directory.

An executive in the local branch of the bank that holds the mortgage on your house might be able to recommend an architect. The local insurance broker who arranged the insurance on your house may be able to suggest a good architect. So may your real estate lawyer.

You may have seen some houses in the area undergoing major alterations that impressed you favorably. The architect's name is often posted at the site. You should also ask the owner a few questions. Anybody whose house you admire should be willing to tell you who designed the changes and even invite you inside. Find out whether a general contractor was employed and, if so, ask for his/her name. Was the G.C. punctual; did he/she return calls; was the work done on schedule; and was the total cost reasonable? If a G.C. was not employed, ask who did the carpentry. The carpenter is the most important subcontractor on a private house renovation. If you are given the carpenter's name, ask the same general questions about his/her reliability and costs.

Local friends and neighbors may also have some recommendations. After you've developed a list of architects, the process of elimination begins. Some local architectural firms may not be available for private house renovations. However, many smaller firms and individual architects will be pleased to work with you. They should be contacted.

First, make some cost-free inquiries. Architects are licensed professionals. Check with the licensing body in your state. Find out how long the architects on your list have been licensed. You want somebody who has had experience providing solutions to problems like yours. You will look into this further but for the moment you want to get an idea of the general experience of the architects on your list.

Call the ones who pass muster and arrange to see each of them briefly at their respective offices. Explain what you're planning but make no commitment. Tell the architect who recommended him or her and ask whether there would be any fee for a brief meeting for the purpose of getting better acquainted. There shouldn't be any charge for this.

Shopping for an architect is much like shopping for a lawyer and the personal aspects of the relationship are as important. Let the architect know that you are not seeking advice but deciding whom to hire to work with you on your house. The architect should have drawings and photographs to show you of other houses he/she has worked on in the area. Ask for some references of clients for whom the architect did work similar to the project you have in mind. The architect you choose should have experience with precisely this kind of job. In the course of these meetings with architects, you will occasionally have an unfavorable personal reaction to a particular architect. Trust your instincts. If you don't think you can work well with any of these people, shorten your list accordingly.

Call the presumably satisfied clients. Be prepared to listen carefully. If they were pleased with the architect's work, they will say so clearly; if they weren't, they may be reluctant to discuss it with you. Try to determine what was done for the clients, whether they were pleased with the job and whether they, the architect or a general contractor supervised the project. If a general contractor, ask whether the architect recommended the G.C. and whether they were pleased with the G.C. Also, try to get a general idea as to whether they were unpleasantly surprised with the cost of the project. If the client liked the work done, ask whether it would be possible to look at what was done to the interior of the house. In any event, you will have gotten the addresses of the satisfied clients from the architect and can always look at the exterior work.

By the time you've completed these preliminaries, your list will be pared to perhaps three or four names at most. Call these architects. Tell them you would like to have them look at your house. Make it clear that this is not a commitment to hire their services but that you are seriously considering doing so. Ask them whether they would charge a fee to meet with you and discuss the work to be done and, if so, how much the fee might be. A local architect will probably charge between zero and $100 for this consultation at current prices and it's money well spent.

However, as it's your money, you may want to try to limit these fees by setting the appointments in the order in which the architect and his/her work impressed you, by pruning the list, and by asking those who intend to charge you whether the fee would be required if you hire their services. I am of two minds about this fee. Ordinarily, I don't like to pay for shopping if I don't buy. However, you've already presumably had one free introductory meeting; this time the architect will be visiting you, requiring more of his/her time for the round trip, and you will be getting ideas, advice and suggestions.

The purpose of the meeting at your house is to give the architect an opportunity to see the scope of the project; to become acquainted with the present and future needs and desires of those who will be living in the house; to look at the structure of the building, to become aware of its age and condition and that of its electrical, plumbing, heating and cooling systems; and to see the land surrounding the house. The architect should be asking questions of you and the others who will be using the house regularly so as to become familiar with living patterns, the priorities you and the others assign to the various aspects of the renovation, and budgetary constraints.

There should be a free flow of information and ideas. The architect will probably have suggestions and may even express an approach or "philosophy." It's important that you and the others who will be living in the house feel comfortable with the architect's attitude. Listen to the architect's ideas about materials, lighting, the utilization of spaces and the style of the project. Be as specific as you like about what you want to accomplish but give the architect some room in which to surprise you with ideas of his/her own. For best results, treat the architect as a professional person, an independent contractor, not simply as somebody who carries out orders. If there is a basic conflict or even a clear difference of opinion on the style of the work to be done, don't hire the architect. With the right architect, you should feel a sense of anticipation, of expectation and excitement.

If you're pleased with the initial meeting with one or more architects, they will probably suggest some preliminary sketches. These costs are minimal and well spent. Have you ever heard anybody complain about spending too much money in planning their renovation? It's the lack of planning that creates inflated costs and much cause for repentance. The idea is to avoid the major mistakes not to have to learn to live with them. Good planning will not only enhance your enjoyment of the house, it will also add to its value.

When you have narrowed the choice of architect to one or two, you will probably want to get a more specific feel for what the architect has in mind before you make a commitment. These specifics will be developed in another meeting, at which time the architect will have some sketches to show you, some choices of materials to discuss and some ideas about costs. The architect you choose will be a licensed professional with solid experience in planning and designing projects like yours. You will have seen other such projects he/she handled successfully and have spoken with satisfied clients. With all of these as givens, the final choice will probably be guided by how comfortably you think you can work with the architect and how much you like the architect's ideas for your project.

At this stage you have some additional choices to make before you formally engage the services of the architect. You will want to decide whether all of the work should be done at the same time or in separate stages, how it should be supervised and perhaps how it should be financed. Some projects lend themselves to being handled piecemeal in that the separable parts can be completed by people in a single profession or trade. For example, you can build a deck, install a pool, repair or replace a roof and do other such jobs without having to coordinate the work outside of a single craft. Other jobs, however, such as adding a bathroom, changing the heating and cooling systems, building fireplaces, reshaping spaces and changing their lighting require the services of two or more crafts. The more crafts, the more collaborative the effort, the more complicated the timing of the work becomes. Each unexpected delay creates its own domino effect on the rest of the job. These delays are inconvenient and they can also be expensive. If you choose to complete the project at one time and it's complicated and involves a number of crafts, you must decide how to handle the effective supervision of the work. This will be addressed shortly.

At this point you have presumably selected an architect to design your renovation and you have reached general agreement on the work to be done. You and the architect must put your agreement in writing and sign it. You must have the protection of well-drawn contracts in every project like the one contemplated. Much more is at stake in a renovation than the costs of materials and labor. An incompetent job can seriously damage your house. If money you paid is not distributed to the people for whom it was intended, they may put liens on your property. People may be injured while working on the job and your insurance may not cover these risks. Well-drawn contracts not only protect you from these and other risks, they also tend to raise the general level of performance of the other signatories.

Ask the architect whether he/she would prefer to draw the agreement or have your lawyer do it. The architect has form contracts (or can copy them) and so does your lawyer. The latter, however, will use forms that favor you or can make the suggested changes in the architect's contract. This will cost about $50 at current prices. The reason you're willing to spend $50 on the lawyer's services instead of fifty cents for a form is that, first, a real estate lawyer should be able to draft a better contract for you than the one printed on the form (if only because the form is a given from the outset) and second, you want the architect (and everybody else on the project with whom you will execute an agreement) to know that you have a lawyer waiting in the wings. It sets a good tone for the relationship.

The agreement with the architect may be tailored to your needs and preferences. The architect may only make sketches and suggestions or he/she may provide all the drawings, advise you on choices of materials, colors, indoor and outdoor treatments of spaces and lighting, estimate costs and priorities, recommend a general contractor (if any), supervise the G.C. or even supervise the project to ensure that the plan is properly executed. If you need or want other consultants, the architect can make recommendations.

Before you sign the agreement with the architect, you should make the important decision of whether or not to hire a general contractor. As a rule, the more complicated the work to be done, the more people involved and the less experienced you are in supervising such an undertaking, the more you need the services of a general contractor. If you're not a seasoned pro at restoring or renovating a house and don't have some special talent for coordinating the work schedules of many people who tend to be a bit independent and often speak in a language for which you lack even a mail-order Rosetta stone, and you'd like to get the job done right the first time without going into bankruptcy or a sanitorium, a good general contractor is the next key person to consider. Using the analogy of putting on a Broadway play, if your architect is the playwright, your G.C. is the director. The right G.C. can take the architect's plans, cost out the materials specified, develop a work schedule, hire the people to carry it out, give you a start date and a completion date, hold you and your house harmless with his/her own insurance and supervise and underwrite the entire job.

Some general contractors, however, will defraud you of substantial sums of money. They will order and approve cheaper-grade materials than those specified in your contract with them and cut corners in the way the work is done. They will employ less-skilled (and less-expensive) personnel than agreed. Instead of hiring a master plumber, your work may be done by an apprentice. Instead of a master electrician who is a longtime member of the IBEW (International Brotherhood of Electrical Workers), your house may be receiving the best efforts of a nonunion person who only recently learned about solder in a high school shop class, before dropping out. General contractors routinely manage substantial sums for people who know little or nothing about construction. The opportunities for unjust enrichment are all too often irresistible.

Departments of Consumer Affairs all over the country have files bulging with anguished complaints about general contractors. Ms. Shirley Goldinger, the Los Angeles County Director of Consumer Affairs, described how some contractors systematically preyed on elderly homeowners. Many of these homeowners had bought their houses decades earlier, for perhaps $10,000 or $15,000. The houses had appreciated over the years to the point that they were worth many times their purchase price. Dishonest contractors would then sell these elderly people, whose principal, often sole, asset was their house, such improvements as a new roof, new siding or central air-conditioning, with the house as collateral to assure payment for the work done.

The work was intentionally substandard. The contractor would ignore the complaints. The homeowner would withhold payment and the contractor would foreclose his mechanic's lien on the property. The customer would either pay the bill or incur wasteful legal costs and fees defending the suit. Either way, the elderly homeowners were pressured into spending large sums of money for little or nothing, accompanied by much anxiety and disappointment. An isolated example? This particular scam became so widespread in Los Angeles, the Department of Consumer Affairs used to send teams of investigators into certain sections of the county to ask homeowners whether they'd recently signed a contract for home improvements.

Contractors in other parts of the country also have shoe boxes densely packed with hundred-dollar bills planted under the radishes in their gardens. I was told this case history by Ms. Esther K. Shapiro, the director of the Detroit Consumer Affairs Department. A hardworking, practical nurse signed a contract to have her kitchen remodeled and for some minor improvements to be made on a covered porch. Under a Federal Trade Commission rule, if somebody sells you something in your residence that costs $25 or more, you have three days in which to change your mind and cancel the purchase. There are some exceptions to the rule. The three-day cooling-off period does not cover contracts for insurance, securities, real estate or emergency home repairs. There are some other wrinkles in the law so it's important to be well advised in a specific case.

In any event, this Detroit woman's contract was covered by the federal three-day cooling-off rule. Her contract called for cabinets, flooring, a dropped ceiling and a little work on the porch. New appliances were not included. She soon discovered she could have a comparable job done for about $4,000, considerably less than the $10,000 price called for in the contract she had been induced to sign. She'd signed her contract on a Friday and the next afternoon her kitchen flooring was being removed. She attempted to cancel the contract at that time but was told it was too late as the work had already begun.

The job was completed. The woman found it totally unsatisfactory and complained to the Detroit DCA. The department investigated. Ms. Shapiro inspected the work herself, in the presence of the company manager and his lawyer. "Cabinets didn't meet. You couldn't open one door because it interfered with other doors. The floor slanted. It was a terrible job."

The lawyer suggested a compromise. The company would redo the work and add some items not in the original contract. The woman considered the offer and decided she didn't want the contractor to do any further work in her house. At that point, Ms. Shapiro spoke: "This contract is void. You violated her rights under the three-day cooling-off period rule. She doesn't owe you anything." Score one for the nurse, zero for the shoe box.

How, then, assuming you need a general contractor, should you go about hiring one who will deliver a high-quality job, on time, at a fair price, and without incident? First, cover the same ground you plowed looking for your architect. Get some recommendations from knowledgeable people who have a natural interest in your success with the project but no vested interest in your hiring the recommended G.C. Add to this list the names of the general contractors you discovered when you were shopping for an architect. Check with the local Better Business Bureau. Find out the volume and types of complaints they have in their files against the general contractors on your list and ask how the complaints were resolved. Make the same inquiries of the relevant licensing body, trade association and regulatory agency, if any. Find out how long the contractors have been in business. The county clerk's office can usually supply this information and the local Better Business Bureau can probably supplement it.

This process should narrow your list. Visit the contractors on your short list at their offices. Discuss your planned renovation. Ask about similar jobs the contractor has done locally and get the names of at least three satisfied clients you may contact.

Ask these clients how the work held up. Visit them. Note the presence or absence of indications of high-quality work. This will shorten your list further. Without putting too much pressure on the question, ask your architect to recommend two or three general building contractors. Mention the fact that you're making other inquiries, too. The architect will presumably recommend people with whom he/she has worked satisfactorily and this is a plus, but you don't want to put the architect off if you hire somebody else.

General building contractors require a license in most cities and towns in this country. Ask your architect if this requirement applies to you. If it does, be certain the G.C. you hire is licensed. This will not guarantee your satisfaction with the work done but it assures a minimum of competence and gives you greater leverage if a dispute arises. Give a copy of your plans to each of the general building contractors on your list and ask them to estimate the total cost. Be as specific as you can about the materials to be used and the appliances to be installed but allow for suggestions from the G.C. Ask for a separate estimate for any changes he/she suggests, as well as an estimate for the job as you outlined it. Ask for samples of materials. To be meaningfully compared, the bids should be based on the same plans and materials.

You will probably be most interested in the mid-range bids. Unusually low bids may indicate a misinterpretation of your plans or foreshadow problems about the actual materials to be used, the quality of the work or the reliability of the schedule. Unless there is sufficient justification in a rare case, high bids may be eliminated for obvious reasons. Cost estimates that begin high usually climb vertically as the work progresses.

Your real estate lawyer should scrutinize every line of the contract with the G.C. and approve all the changes before you sign it. The contract form should be one approved by the American Institute of Architects. A Department of Consumer Affairs may also be able to give you a copy of a good home improvement contract. You should check your contract against one provided by a local DCA. If there is no local DCA, get a copy of a good contract from a DCA in the same state as the house you're renovating.

The contract should include the contractor's license number and a detailed description of the work to be done. Incorporate the architect's plans, drawings and specifications in the contract. Spell out the precise materials, quality and brand names and even the manufacturer's order numbers. Specify a start date and a completion date for the work to be done.

The payment schedule should provide an ample holdback to help assure performance and a clause permitting you to apply unpaid amounts to hiring somebody else if the work is not completed on schedule or is interrupted by a specified number of days. You may also include a penalty for slow work. The plans and specifications may not be changed without your written consent. The contractor must be properly insured for property damage and personal injuries and this insurance should hold you harmless. All work permits must be obtained by, and at the expense of, the G.C. and all codes must be complied with. You also want to specify the qualifications and certifications of the people who will actually do the work. I would insist on an IBEW electrician. The contractor must also protect you from mechanics' liens of any subcontractors. This would assure that if you pay the G.C., but the latter fails to pay one or more of the subcontractors, you would not be liable to any such third parties.

All the guarantees and warranties covering parts, materials and labor must be set forth in writing and in detail. The parts and materials should be specified as new. Try to pay as little as possible in advance. You want to pay after material is delivered and work has commenced. The G.C. has lots of credit with suppliers. You prefer to pay for completed work. The acceptable compromise is a schedule of payments that provides significant holdbacks coupled with specific start and end dates and a penalty for slow work. All permits must be in the name of the contractor, not in your name, so that the G.C., not you, is liable for violations.

There are a number of ways to pay the contractor. Avoid the cost-plus contract, an arrangement by which you pay for all the labor and materials plus an additional percentage of this total or an additional fixed sum of money. Cost-plus arrangements provide no assurance of the total cost of the project and no incentive to the contractor to do the work efficiently. You are forced to rely on the good faith of the G.C. in his/her financial arrangements with several subcontractors and suppliers. You have no long-term business relationship with the G.C. on which to base this trust. You also have no easy way to discover bill padding and are only too likely to be unpleasantly surprised with the total cost of the project. This is the kind of contract our federal government has made with hundreds of suppliers and it's the reason a forty-nine-cent spare part costs $174.

You may expect to do better with a fixed-fee contract. You pay a total price for all of the work done, which total includes the general contractor's estimated profit. Except for changes you decide on or approve, this controls the total cost of the project. However, you must be careful to assure that you are getting the grade and type of materials and labor for which you contracted. Your architect can help you with this supervision in order that the work follows the plan.

The general contractor is extremely important to your project. You can have an excellent plan and use the best materials but unless skilled people execute the plan with distinction and utilize the materials properly, you can be constructing an expensive pile of junk. The G.C. not only assembles and manages the people who do the work, but the G.C. is also responsible to you if anything goes wrong. Without this unified control of the project, every little problem may be escalated into a major battle at your expense in money, time and anguish. Each delay or change affects another part of the job. Each trade or craft can attempt to shift the responsibility for poor performance. It's a quagmire. Instead of a seamless whole, you have nothing but seams at any of which your project may easily fall apart.

The G.C. is the director of your project. If you or your architect would like to make a suggestion as the work progresses, don't discuss it with the plumber, the carpenter, the mason or the electrician. Producers and authors don't talk to members of the cast about script changes or how the part is being interpreted. They talk to the director. The G.C., like any good director, has special channels of communication with the cast you and your architect don't have. The craft and trade people, like actors, have their own languages and preferred ways of communicating. Some actors like to discuss motivation; others prefer to defer these conversations until dinner or find it easier to exchange ideas over drinks. Still others would rather work on the problem by themselves after they are made aware, by the merest hint, or most minimal gesture, that a problem exists.

You should have an agreed payment schedule with the contractor that enables you to hold back the last 10–20 percent of the total cost for a minimum of thirty days after the work is completed. You may then use this period of time for inspection and corrections. Only when you're satisfied with the completed work should you sign a completion certificate. However, don't wait until the job is completed to discuss any reservations you may have about the way the work is being done. Meet with the G.C. regularly. Review the work, the schedule and any actual or potential problems of which you're aware. Your architect should also make suggestions. The contract you signed with the architect should include some consultation time for the architect to review the progress of the work.

If you intend to borrow money to pay for the renovation, let your bank see the contract with the G.C. before you sign it. Include a clause that requires the contractor to leave your house and land broom-clean after completion of the job and to keep the place clean and reasonably free of debris as the work progresses. Before final payment, the contractor must furnish you with an itemized, signed statement of the work done and specifying that all the materials used were new. The G.C. should also warrant that all the work is free of defects and conforms to the specifications of your plan, and that if any defect in materials or labor arises within an agreed period, the contractor agrees to make timely repairs and replacements at no additional cost to you.

If you have a local building inspection department, you should have the work approved and receive a statement that your house complies in all ways with local codes and regulations before you make the final payment to the G.C. If there is no such department, the local bank that holds your mortgage or those of your neighbors can recommend an engineer for the same purpose. With the project successfully completed as planned, you are a decorated veteran, ready to celebrate and to enjoy your first unbroken night's sleep in weeks.

☐ Buying a Car: How to Drive a Bargain

The economic impact of the automobile on the U.S. economy is so gargantuan it can be adequately pictured only by aerial photography. Statistical data do not, of course, tell the whole story, but to cite one impressive number, the cost of buying, maintaining, repairing, insuring and fueling cars in this country costs about $100 million per day at this writing, and is rising. Most of this money is spent on the purchase of new and used cars, and in virtually each and every such transaction, the buyer is in an overmatch with the seller that almost invariably results in the payment of too much for too little. This is an inherently unsatisfactory position for buyers and a source of much displeasure. In fact, complaints about cars rank number one among all complaints to the Federal Trade Commission.

Let me concede early on that not all car salespersons are convicted criminals. That would be an unwarranted assumption. However, it can hardly be coincidental that this particular calling has supplied more scamster Hall of Famers and more holders of the coveted Golden Fleecing Life Achievement Award than the next twenty categories combined, dwarfing its nearest rival, lawyers, like Gulliver among the Lilliputians. Nor is it for naught that the car salesperson is as finely etched a twentieth-century folk character, as well observed and clearly defined, as was Punchinello or Pantalone.

Suffice it to say that trying to break even with these people is like trying to break even with a three-card monte dealer who also places your bets for you. Your objective in buying a car must therefore be more modest and more feasible than breaking even. Like other right-minded buyers, you would like to make a fair deal that gives you what you want and need when you buy a car and gives the seller a fair, but not excessive or exorbitant, profit. The fact that such a reasonable objective is so rarely attained requires that you remain alert and observe good practice at all points of contact with these freebooters.

The process of buying a car usually begins with a comparison of your needs, desires and finances with what's available in the marketplace, followed by a narrowing of focus to perhaps two or three makes and models. For this purpose, get the annual auto issue of *Consumer Reports.* This is usually the April issue of the magazine. It costs $2.00, is in great demand and usually sells out quickly, but is widely available in libraries. It is the best single source of car-buying information I know of and is chock-full of good advice about how to buy, how to bargain, which options are recommended in each make and model (including their advantages, disadvantages and wholesale and retail prices), how to finance a car, car-crash results, dealer costs, judgments on more than a hundred new models (with test results on road and track), plus specific recommendations, pro and con, on used cars.

Another resource Consumers Union (the publishers of *Consumer Reports*) offers is a computer printout service that shows the dealer cost and list price of the base car and every individual piece of optional equipment offered (with CU's recommendations), as well as the destination charge for new cars by make, model and style. The cost for this service in 1984 was $9 for one car, $17 for two and $24 for three cars. By adding the dealer cost for the options already on the car in the showroom to the base price plus the destination charge, you arrive at the dealer cost of the car.

The dealer is also probably paying interest to finance the car and has some other overhead expense in dealer prep. However, the actual cost (as distinguished from the cost the salesperson alleges) of these items is offset by about a 2 percent rebate from the manufacturer on new cars. In any event, don't be misled by inflated claims for overhead and dealer prep. Point out that the dealer rebate defrays these costs and you don't intend to pay for them again.

It is obviously extremely useful to know the dealer's cost for the car being offered to you. In addition, if you want to add or delete options for that make and model, you know what to add or subtract in each case. It's a little like knowing your opponent's hole card in a head-to head, five-card stud game, but don't become complacent or overconfident. You will be up against batteries of pros and superpros and, before you finally emerge with a signed contract that represents a good deal on the car you want, equipped as you want it, you will hear much puffery and many self-serving declarations and deceptive statements, reminiscent of the streets of Pamplona during the running of the bulls.

You need more information before you're ready to go shopping. First, you should know whether any of the cars that interest you has a "corporate twin." Such a twin is essentially the same car with a different name. If so, you have an additional source of supply. The *Consumer Reports Annual Auto Issue* also lists these corporate twins. You should also know the wholesale and retail prices of your car if you plan to sell it or trade it in. For the wholesale price, consult a current copy of the "Blue Book" (the *National Automobile Dealers Association Official Used Car Guide*) or call your bank and ask a loan officer. Your bank or a public library can probably supply you with a reference copy. The retail price of your car may be estimated by looking at newspaper advertisements of used-car dealers.

You also need to know the cost and availability of financing the purchase of the car. In general terms, a "personal loan" is about the most expensive and least desirable way to finance. A car loan from a bank is cheaper and many banks offer their own customers a preferential interest rate. A credit union loan is still less costly. You might also consider borrowing against marginable securities from your broker (you'll pay between ½ and 2½ percent over prime, compounded monthly) or of borrowing against the cash value of life insurance, which is probably the least expensive way to borrow money from strangers. Armed with the facts and a verbal commitment from a loan officer, if needed, you may then easily compare these terms with those offered by the car dealer and make an informed decision.

After these preliminaries are out of the way, have an early dinner in midweek, set aside more time than you think you'll need and visit a showroom. No matter how good a negotiator you are, remember that you are not on your own turf and that the automobile salesperson you are engaging is a real pro supervised by superpros. A veteran car salesperson has probably sold three or four hundred cars by the time you waltz in and he/she has heard it all. This veteran is also familiar with every sales technique and trick in the game. The approach suggested here is designed to reduce the house advantage; no approach can eliminate it entirely.

You chose to visit the showroom during the middle of the week because most sales are made on weekends, when demand is high, crowds are lively and good deals for buyers are in short supply. In midweek, the action is slow. The end of the month is also a favorable time for buyers because the sales force is rated on its performance for the month. Those at the bottom of the sales chart face a certain amount of heat from the sales manager and their continued employment may even hinge on making a sale. Your business may thus take on an unwonted importance. Some experts also recommend you go shopping for a car after the first post-Christmas storm, when Christmas shopping has depleted most budgets, people are hunkered down at home or visiting with the family and demand is slack.

You chose to eat dinner early and visit the showroom at your regular dinnertime because the wiliest veterans among the sales force (those you'd prefer to avoid) usually usurp these favored dining hours, relegating the younger and more inexperienced barracudas to minding the store at these times. They will eat later, when some of the good desserts and daily specials are no longer available. You've already eaten and will face your salesperson when the double hunger for food and sales can cloud judgment even to the point of accepting a fair deal.

Buying a new car is a complex transaction. There are a number of separable parts to the deal. There is the purchase of the base car. There is the options package. If you have a car to be sold, there is the possible trade-in. There is also the possible financing of the purchase with or through the dealer. Each element represents a profit opportunity for the seller.

The salesperson will concede a deal point on one of these elements and then try to make it up in spades on some other element of the deal. You must be aware of these attempts in order to keep the total profit reasonable. The more elements you can control, the more control you will be able to exert on the total deal. The seller will also try to control the elements so as to increase the total profit. If the salesperson seems to be taking complete control of the sale, you can try a simple farewell address in lieu of twelve more rounds toe to toe.

"I don't want to slug it out. I'm prepared to buy a car today." This will get the salesperson's attention. Then make your bid. "I'll give you $9,850 for this car as it stands, even though I don't want every one of the options on the car." Pause for a moment and, if there is no response from the salesperson, walk to the door at your regular gait.

The salesperson should be reluctant to see a customer who's ready to buy "today" walk out the door.

"Look, the best price I can give you is only a little higher —$10,150. It's a bargain at that price, and if you don't buy it, lots of other people will."

"I don't want to be rude, but at that price, you'll have to find somebody else."

You've stopped to say this and the salesperson is now at your side. The usual technique here, as the price of the car seems important to you, is to try to punch up the total profit by finding some other element of the deal to work on while leaving the actual price of the car undetermined. This allows the salesperson to dance back and forth, setting up a profitable deal for the seller and leaving you out of control of every element. To facilitate these transitions, the salesperson may introduce a little patter about the sales incentive contest he/she is close to winning, with which your help would be most appreciated, or you will hear some other irrelevant tale designed to soften you up or feel you out. Feel free to interrupt this.

"Let's cut to the chase. I'm willing to pay $9,850 for the car as it stands. Yes or no?"

You may then expect to hear some hypothetical questions

that don't commit to anything and don't answer your question.

"If I can sell you the car for $10,000, and it won't be easy to get the sales manager to agree, will you finance it here?"

The proper responses to questions followed by the word "if" are answers followed by the same word.

"If the car is $9,850, I would consider financing here but the terms would have to make sense."

If this sparring becomes uncomfortably protracted, take out your card or a piece of paper on which you've previously written your name and telephone number and say, "I'm ready to buy the car right now for $9,850. If you can't sell it to me at that price now, call me when you can."

Needless to say, this is not a commitment and the salesperson knows it. The latter may get the message and make the sale, relying on his/her ability to punch up the profit while the contract is being executed, or you may have to leave without making a deal. Don't be disappointed. Your time will be well compensated when you do buy the car you want at a reasonable price. Besides, you may be surprised to get a call in a day or two from this salesperson or one of the dealer's "closers." In any case, you know the dealer cost of the car and every optional piece of equipment on it and you know what represents a reasonable markup. You don't have to make a bad deal and, unless you have to have one of the hottest cars of the year, there are many more cars out there than there are buyers. You have the ultimate control in that you don't have to buy anything from this dealer, while every unsold car in the showroom or on the lot costs the seller additional overhead expense.

If you have a car to trade in and are able to negotiate a fair price on the new car, you will probably be offered a ridiculously low price for your old car. Before discussing the terms on the trade-in, write down the price you negotiated for the new car and put it in plain sight. It isn't binding on the dealership but it *is* a useful reminder of a verbally agreed price. It's entirely within your control whether you will trade in your old car as part of the deal. You also control whether to finance through the dealer as well as how and when to reveal the amount of your down payment. To illustrate how all of these factors may be managed to your advantage, assume that you've done all the preliminary information gathering and the comparative shopping and are now ready to play a serious game of "Let's Make a Deal."

To review the bidding, you've had an early dinner and have plenty of time. It's the middle of the week, three days after Christmas and the day after the first big storm of the season. You have an appointment with the young salesperson you met a couple of weeks ago when you were doing your comparative shopping.

You won't make the mistake of underestimating him/her and you know that absolutely nothing he/she says is legally binding unless it's contained in the written contract and signed. You also know that you won't be given such a contract until the dealership wants you to have it. This means that you will have to be prepared to meet not only this salesperson but a larger cast of characters before the deal is made.

You are a serious buyer, not one of the lunchtime drop-ins idling some time away before returning to work or you wouldn't have come back by appointment. You also have a car to trade in, which increases the profit potential of the deal. You want to establish the price of the new car equipped to your order. This should be done early in the negotiation for maximum leverage. The other major elements of the deal are more easily controlled by you; i.e., whether to trade in your car, whether to finance through the dealership and how large the down payment. Each of these elements is a profit opportunity to the seller and you may be able to manage them so as to obtain additional concessions on the price of the new car in order to keep the total cost reasonable.

The salesperson will be attempting to feel out the full scope of the deal before committing to the price of the new car. You will be asked a number of questions designed to develop this information. Your attitude should be that everything is possible if you like the price of the new car.

"Will you be trading in your old car, Mr./Ms. Cooper?"

"That's entirely possible—you are keeping all options open—"but I want to find out first where I'll be buying the new car."

You don't want to eliminate any category of potential profit as this will tend to stiffen the terms of the purchase. Besides, if the dealer is close on the terms of the financing, you may decide to give them some additional profit on the financing if the cost of the new car is sufficiently attractive and you get a reasonable price for your old car. Some states permit you to subtract the price of the trade-in from the price of the new car for sales tax purposes, eliminating the state sales tax on the amount you get for your old car if you trade it in at the time of purchasing the new car. This would narrow the gap somewhat between the wholesale and retail price of your old car and make the trade-in a bit more attractive.

The salesperson may offer to take you for a test drive if your interest in a particular car seems genuine. The idea is to get you more sensorially involved with the car and thus to heighten its sales appeal. You don't mind getting the feel of the car, although you know a short "test drive" won't be especially revealing. You want the salesperson to invest some more time in making the sale because the more time thus invested, the more apt he/she is to want to realize some profit on the investment. This should make it a little easier for you to lever the price into an acceptable range. However, don't allow yourself to be taken for a ride in a souped-up "demonstrator" model. You want to drive the car you're considering buying or an exact duplicate off the floor. If the license plate says "dealer," don't get into the car.

The average profit on a new car bought in this country is $700–$1,200 but you can do better than this. The sticker price already includes a high profit margin, perhaps 20 percent above wholesale. Many dealers will attempt to add a few hundred dollars to this excessive price for "dealer prep," explaining how carefully they inspect and prepare the car before offering it for sale. Don't even consider paying for dealer prep. The suggested retail price means exactly that and is already too high.

You may insist on buying the car you want equipped with only the options you want. If it's not in stock, the dealer can order it from the factory. However, it's more efficient for the dealer to sell you a car already in the showroom. You may be willing to accommodate the dealer by taking a car on hand with an option like a power trunk-lid lock release at a cost of maybe $35, but it's a mistake to pay $600 for the AM/FM ETR stereo with seek/scan cassette and graphic equalizer. If you're interested in good sound, you will do better in quality and price by buying the components than by accepting the equipment installed by the automobile manufacturer. You might also consider the greater likelihood of burglary that good sound equipment can create. In any case, get an inexpensive, factory installed AM/FM with speakers, because (1) you want a radio; (2) it will be easier to sell the car if it has a radio; and (3) you will also get the wiring system so that, if you want better sound, you can install it more easily. Exotic options often create exotic repair bills, but if you must buy a loaded car, don't pay the retail price for the options package. There is much fat there to be trimmed before giving the dealer a fair profit.

You may recall how counterproductive I suggested it was, in dealing with an insurance adjuster, simply to state what you thought was a reasonable estimate, and that this approach would net you less than if your initial estimate was on the high side. The ritual requires the claimant to come in high, the adjuster to feign disbelief and counteroffer low and for the two sides to dance toward each other according to their own personal rhythms. Buying a car is a similar kind of negotiation but it's complicated by the fact that there are several divisible parts to the car transaction, so you must be careful to prevent any gains you make on a particular part from being lost somewhere else.

You should be able to buy the average car for no more than the dealer cost, including the destination charge, plus about $300 but only if you observe the ritual (and good practice). So let the salesperson do his/her job. Let the music play and wear your dancing shoes. Go for the test drive. Admit you're interested but don't give the impression you must have the car. In fact, if you take a friend with you, you may even heighten the drama by having your friend disagree on whether to buy the car.

As the dance continues, the differences are narrowed. You offer the dealer about $100 over cost and transportation, say $8,800. The salesperson tells you it can't be done and makes another attempt to find out whether you plan to trade in your car and finance the purchase through the dealership. You remain noncommittal and keep your options open. The seller may then quote a price for the car somewhat under the sticker price.

"If I'm willing to trade in my car at a reasonable price, will you sell me the car for $8,800?"

"How much do you want for your car?"

You know your car wholesales for about $1,550 and needs a minor repair, at a cost of about $50, for a net wholesale price of about $1,500.

"$1,800."

You are deliberately high. The salesperson will probably tell you they already have too many unsold used cars and that the market is slow, point out a list of repairs needed on your car and offer perhaps $1,200 if you pay $9,200 for the car. You are $500 apart at the moment. You are willing to pay $9,000 minus $1,500 for your car, or $7,500. The salesperson wants $9,200 for the new car and is offering $1,200 for your car, or $8,000. You now select the price that's more out of line, in this case, the $1,200 offer for your car, for remediation.

"I know this car wholesales for $1,550 and needs a repair that will cost no more than $50. It's in great shape otherwise and you can probably turn it over quickly for at least $2,000 or wait and get even more. I've seen the car on used-car lots in much worse shape for $2,300."

The salesperson may say he/she will talk to the sales manager but doubts this price will be approved. You proceed as if $1,500 is agreed.

"Okay. With $1,500 for my car I can give you $8,900."

"I may be able to get the sales manager to approve $1,450 and $9,100 if we handle the financing. How much of a down payment are you planning on making?"

The question of the financing is best left open, for the moment. You've covered considerable ground with the salesperson and this is about the point you'll meet the "closer" or the sales manager, a superpro in either case, who will create a number of changes and apparent obstacles in the negotiation you conducted with the salesperson, all designed to punch up the total profit on the deal. This highly skilled specialist will try for complete control of the renegotiation and you'll find lots of numbers jumping all over the page. The closer or sales manager can do the mental arithmetic at about the same speed as an accomplished abacus operator. The way to neutralize this advantage is to say you're slow with numbers, to use a hand calculator you or your friend has brought along for the purpose and to write all the numbers down on a large piece of paper.

You can always create a little insecurity in a seller by taking exception to some of the features in what's being offered for sale. The car has too many optional items on it you don't need or want. It's not roomy enough for your family, especially when you consider how quickly children grow; or it's really a little too big for your needs because you have no family. You're also a little nervous about the color, as it isn't yellow or light green, which are, respectively, two and four times more visible in fog, rain and twilight than dark colors, and hence safer. These objections should be made one at a time when the superpro tries to renegotiate additional profit for the dealership.

Watch the credit terms carefully. The seller usually wants to get as much of a down payment as will assure no risk of loss in the event of repossession and have you finance the rest of the purchase through the dealer. You will usually (but not always) pay a higher rate for this loan than you could obtain from other lenders. However, you can narrow this differential and still make a favorable total deal, which is your objective. In addition, you can always prepay the loan or refinance it elsewhere.

The three factors to watch are the annual percentage rate of interest (APR), the amount of the monthly payment and the number of them. At a given rate of interest, the lower the monthly payment, the longer the term of the loan and the higher the total interest. A loan of $8,000 at an APR of 14 percent works out as follows:

# of Payments	Amount	Total Interest
24	$384	$1,218
36	273	1,843
48	219	2,494
60	186	3,169

At a 13% APR, the comparable figures are as follows:

# of Payments	Amount	Total Interest
24	$380	$1,128
36	270	1,704
48	215	2,302
60	182	2,922

Note that the most important element affecting the total interest you pay is the *length* of the loan *not* the APR. A 36-month loan of $8,000 at 14 percent costs $1,843 in interest, as against $3,169 for a five-year loan at the same rate, whereas a 1 percent difference in APR (from 14 to 13 percent) involves a difference in cost of no more than $3.00 or $4.00 per month.

Let's say you know that the wholesale price of the car and optional equipment you want, added to the destination charge, sales tax and license fee is $9,000. Given the condition of the market, you expect to pay about $400 above this price, or about $9,400. You also know that the wholesale price of your car, minus the cost of repairs, is $2,000. You plan to make a $2,400 down payment and finance approximately $5,-000 for 36 months. Your bank or another source has supplied a table of interest costs and monthly payments, showing that a $5,000 loan for 36 months works out as follows:

APR	Monthly Payment	Total Interest
10%	$161	$ 808
11%	164	893

APR	Monthly Payment	Total Interest
12%	166	979
13%	168	1,065
14%	171	1,152
15%	173	1,240
16%	176	1,329

Once you and the dealership are close on the price of the new car and are at least in the same county on the trade-in value of your car, you are ready to discuss financing. You begin by offering *only* the trade-in value of your car, assuming you get its approximate wholesale value (minus needed repairs). You ask what the APR and the monthly payments would be for a three-year loan on the balance. If your car has sufficient trade-in value, these figures will be supplied. Otherwise, you will be told that some cash will also be required. If, for example, you need to add a minimum of $500, you will be given the APR and the monthly payments on a three-year loan for the balance.

This is your cue to object to the size of the monthly payments. The seller will suggest that the payments can be reduced by extending the loan to 48 months (increasing your interest costs and their profit). You multiply the monthly payment by 48 and express your unhappiness with the total cost of the loan. The seller will explain that the only way to reduce the total cost with these smaller monthly payments is to increase your down payment. You reply that a lower APR would also help and are told this is the best rate they can offer. You then make a number of conditional offers (one at a time), each one raising the down payment modestly. These incremental increases in your down payment (toward the $2,400 you had in mind originally) are "concessions" on your part and you expect some corresponding "give" from the seller (toward your objective, a reasonable deal).

"If I put up $1,000 in addition to the trade-in, I need a better price for my car."

You will gradually make it clear that you won't take less than the wholesale value of your car, minus necessary repairs, and that you know exactly what that amount is. You also expressly reserve the option not to trade in your car and, indeed, to buy elsewhere. Actually, you are willing to take $50 or $75 less than this figure but this compromise should come at the end of the entire negotiation or you are likely to be making a series of small price concessions that, in the aggregate, will cost you more than necessary and create a less than acceptable total deal.

At this point the seller has spent a considerable amount of time with you and knows you'll sign a contract if the price and terms are reasonable. No dealer wants to see a serious buyer walk out of the showroom. Therefore, the dealer must also make concessions if there is to be a meeting of the minds.

Be careful that a concession on the dealer's part isn't used to induce you to spend money on something you don't want, such as an extended warranty plan, rustproofing, undercoating or perhaps some insurance at an inflated price. Decline these opportunities and point out that you have already made a concession by adding more cash to the down payment. Whether you make a deal at this dealership or somewhere else, unless you absolutely must have a car that is in unusually high demand, relative to supply, you should be able to buy a new car at a reasonable price and on reasonable terms.

Make sure you get a signed, duly authorized contract when the deal is made. Do not leave the showroom without it. Be sure to specify the delivery date in the contract, plus your right to an immediate refund and cancellation of the contract in the event the car isn't delivered by that date, and as specified in the contract. This is especially important if you are buying a car the dealer has to order.

Without this provision in the contract, the dealer may try to renegotiate the contract, to your detriment. You ask about delivery and are given an approximate date, say about five weeks later. You put a deposit on the new car, both sides sign the contract and you then set about selling your car privately. If you fail to provide the clause suggested above, the dealer may keep you waiting indefinitely and then offer you "a great buy on a terrific car that just came in," reopening the entire negotiation. If you sold your car in reliance on the promised delivery date, you are going to be under pressure to buy.

You also want to avoid any possible price increases while you're waiting for delivery. Look for this kind of language in the sales contract and make it clear that you won't buy the car if it's subject to a price increase. If this language isn't deleted and initialed by the dealership, express your intention to go elsewhere and buy the car you want out of another dealer's stock.

A used car may better serve your needs than a new car. About three out of four cars bought by private individuals are used cars and they average less than half the cost of new cars. While there are obvious uncertainties inherent in a used car, a good, well-chosen, late-model one properly inspected by a competent mechanic can deliver excellent value. A new car depreciates almost one third after the first year and almost 60 percent after two years, so the savings are real. In addition, used cars have a published track record of statistical data by which you may assess their mechanical reliability, handling and safety. An excellent source of an enormous amount of such data is a recent edition of *Consumer Reports Guide to Used Cars*. Hundreds of models are included with detailed judgments, recommendations (pro and con) and a wealth of information designed to aid you in making an intelligent choice of a used car.

A more efficient buy than a new car, if shopped wisely, a used car can be particularly efficient for those who own more than one car. Short trips are especially hard on a car's engine. Moving a car from the driveway of your house into the garage after the engine has cooled causes about as much wear on the engine as driving a warmed-up car several hundred highway miles. In fact, under certain conditions, the latter may actually be beneficial. If the less expensive, used car were pressed into service for the short trips, like buying the groceries or dropping the children off at school, this engine wear on your more expensive car could be averted, adding to its longevity.

As was suggested earlier, the "Blue Book," or *National Automobile Dealers Association Official Used Car Guide,* a monthly publication, lists the trade-in and retail prices of used cars. This is a good way to get the handle on the current prices. The "Blue Book" is widely available in libraries, and the loan officer of your bank will probably let you peruse a copy. In addition, classified advertisements of private individuals offering to sell used cars is also a good indication; if you subtract about 15 percent from the prices of non-Japanese cars, you have the approximate wholesale price. The more exotic the car and its features, the more likely it is to require expensive repairs. In general, the best buys are found among selected four-door sedans that are still in production.

There are several major sources of used cars and each has its peculiar advantages and disadvantages. In a private sale, the car may have been owned by a friend or relative or somebody else you know. This relationship may provide a good basis on which to get an accurate history of repairs and maintenance and the general condition of the car. You may expect to pay close to the average of the "Blue Book" trade-in and retail prices. While you may do well on price and even get a fairly reliable car, you will usually spend more time shopping the private market, as you will be considering one car at a time. You will also be buying the car "as is," that is, without any warranty.

New-car dealers charge as much as the traffic will bear and you will pay close to the retail price. However, new-car dealers usually hold for resale only the best cars they take in trade, so you should be buying out of preferred stock. These dealers sell cars of lesser quality they take in trade at auction or to used-car dealers. A reliable new-car dealer, one you or your friends have done business with over the years, can supply a good, late-model used car, albeit slightly on the high side, and give you at least limited written warranty protection.

Used-car dealers usually charge less for their offerings than the same make and model would fetch at a new-car dealership but the quality tends to be much more uneven. This will ordinarily translate into more shopping time and a number of fees spent for inspections by an auto mechanic who found enough wrong with the cars you'd selected to discourage further interest.

Car rental agencies offer quantities of late-model cars for sale to the public. One of the major car renters told me they would sell any car in their fleet. Rental cars usually have relatively high mileage but they are well equipped and regularly maintained. The actual maintenance reports are usually available on these cars and most car rental agencies have entered into agreements with the Federal Trade Commission prohibiting sales of cars that have undergone more than about $750 worth of maintenance and repairs, thus eliminating cars that have been in major accidents.

Rental cars also come with written limited warranties. You should be able to get a warranty for at least 12 months or 12,000 miles on the power train. Although limited, this warranty covers the engine and transmission, sites of expensive repairs. A good, professional inspection should be able to detect most of the other foreseeable problems. If you're interested in buying a used car from a car renter, you may arrange to rent the car for a couple of days, get the feel of it under various driving conditions and also have it inspected. You should be able to deduct the cost of the rental if you buy the car.

Regardless of who the seller is, you need to take some elementary precautions. Always test drive the car. If you're satisfied, have a competent automobile mechanic examine the car in a shop or diagnostic center. You want more than an opinion. You want the mechanic to do a number of tests in a shop sufficiently well equipped to perform them properly. The ability of auto mechanics varies widely. Only a handful of states require mechanics to be licensed and most cannot competently perform the entire range of diagnoses and repairs on all of the mechanical systems in a car. Although certification doesn't guarantee performance, I would choose a mechanic certified by the National Institute for Automotive Service Excellence (NIASE).

Compare the vehicle identification number on the registration form with that on the car's identification plate. They must match and not look as if they've been changed or you're probably looking at a stolen car. If you decide to buy, get all warranties and other representations in writing. You can avoid driving a known safety hazard by calling the Auto Safety Hotline (1-800-404-9393). Ask whether the model car you have has ever been recalled for a safety defect. If so, on your supplying the model, make, year and vehicle identification number of the car, you will be told whether the car was actually brought in to have the safety defect cured. If not, this can be done by any new-car dealer that sells this make automobile, at no cost to you.

Cars are expensive, inefficient, hazardous, environmentally unsound and a major source of discontent. The American public has had a complex, "can't live with it, can't live without it," love-hate relationship with the automobile for more than two generations that seems likely to continue at least until we have something better in general use. In the meantime, we can at least keep the costs reasonable, heed the owner's manual and drive safely and soberly.

☐ Mail Order

Selling products through the United States mails began as a convenient and profitable way of providing farmers and other rural Americans with "store-bought" goods, locally unavailable. Clothing, kitchenware, home furnishings and other products were manufactured in large cities and shipped to people on farms and in small towns in remote locations. The early Sears catalogs became popular symbols of the dreams that money could buy and they were eagerly thumbed by all of the members of the family old enough to read. Used to dealing face to face with the proprietor of the saloon, the owner of the general store and the blacksmith, our American ancestors did not permit distance to eliminate the personal contact between buyer and seller, to which they had become accustomed. Mail orders were often accompanied by long, chatty letters and the goods were delivered with equally long, personal replies.

In recent years, the business of selling by mail has become a major industry. The Sears catalog alone currently generates about $4 billion in annual sales. Total catalog sales in this country exceed $40 billion per year and the total of goods and services purchased in the United States each year as a result of direct response marketing (including telephone, as well as mail, orders) is more than $150 billion, according to the Direct Marketing Association.

Men, women and children throughout the country in big cities, metropolitan suburbs and small towns and villages buy through the mail for a variety of reasons. For some, the anticipation of receiving something of special value addressed to them and delivered to their door or mailbox is emotionally satisfying. Others are caught up in the strong sales appeals of a direct mail campaign, catalog item or broadcast offer. Convenience is the primary motivation of many others. The elderly, the infirm, young children, college students, convalescents, prisoners and many others who live far from urban shopping centers often find shopping by mail a preferable alternative to making do without. The fact that no salesperson will contact them in person or pressure them into buying something is an attractive feature of mail-order buying for many people. For some, price is an important consideration. Then, too, some goods and services are available *only* via mail order and their novelty or uniqueness promotes the sale.

Unfortunately, mail-order selling is one of the major sources of customer complaints. In a study conducted by the Federal Trade Commission (FTC) and participated in by a number of federal, state and local agencies, consumer complaints were analyzed during a six-month test period. "Failure to deliver merchandise that had been paid for was found to be by far the most frequent consumer complaint and complaints against mail-order houses for failure to deliver ranked near the top in terms of the type of business complained about most by consumers."

The President's Office of Consumer Affairs received more than 1,100 consumer complaints concerning mail-order practices in a seven-month period, exceeded in volume only by complaints about automobiles and auto services. Analyses of customer complaints in every region of the country establish ordering by mail a leading source of dissatisfaction among buyers. In a study cited in the *Federal Register* (Vol. 40, No. 214, p. 51582), the San Francisco Bay area reported that the failure to deliver mail-order merchandise was the "most common complaint" received and that the "largest number of complaints concerned mail-order houses." The attorney general of Wisconsin told the Federal Trade Commission that failure to deliver merchandise ranked either first or second in volume of consumer complaints received each year in that state during a four-year period.

The FTC study cited earlier developed a record of more than 10,000 pages of complaints about mail-order sales and it was supplemented by testimony supplied by state and local agencies and consumer groups, as well as more than 3,000 actual complaint letters of dissatisfied customers. The report that followed acknowledged the widespread complaint of nondelivery of goods ordered by mail. After repeated efforts to obtain the merchandise ordered and paid for, mail-order customers all over the country were often disheartened to learn "that the mail-order company had either gone out of business, moved to an unknown address, filed for reorganization or been petitioned into bankruptcy."

"What recourse does a citizen of one state have when doing business with a company in another state?" asked an irate Ohio father, whose children sought his help. "Last winter an ad appeared . . . promoting (lettered) T-shirts. . . . My children pooled their allowance money and a check for $6.50 was sent to (the company). The company cashed the check; however, we have yet to receive the shirts. For the past six months, I have been attempting to get a refund on the shirts—but to no avail. It is a disgrace that business is permitted to cheat the public—and now children seem to be fair play."

The FTC record also underscores the difficulty of obtaining a refund for undelivered goods. "Consumers . . . reported that refunds were made only after numerous requests to the seller, pleas to a governmental agency to intercede and months of waiting. . . ." Many others complained about the practice of some mail-order sellers giving customers credits toward future purchases instead of cash refunds for undelivered merchandise.

Representative Benjamin Rosenthal of New York summarized the potential for abuses in mail-order marketing in his testimony before the FTC in these hearings: "While most mail-order firms are run by honest businessmen who serve their customers quickly and fairly . . . under existing laws the unscrupulous mail-order house can . . . (hide) behind a post office box number and/or a fabricated business name, it can deliver inferior merchandise, or no merchandise at all, disregard consumer complaints and, if things get too uncomfortable, file for bankruptcy or simply leave town. The consumer, with canceled check in hand, is left remedy-less, often after months of frustrated letter writing to consumer groups, Better Business Bureaus, congressmen, the President's adviser and the firm itself."

Customer complaints about mail-order companies are not only numerous, they are also difficult for the buyer to resolve satisfactorily. If you buy something from a local store, you may take your complaint to the seller in person or by telephone and further recourse, if necessary, is relatively easy. The seller is within your reach and that of all of the other dispute-resolving mechanisms our society provides. You also have some familiarity with the local shop and its business practices and may even have seen and touched the goods you itend to buy before you order them. Thus, you may not only make a more informed buying decision, but even more fundamental to your purchase, you know the item you want exists and is immediately available to you.

On the other hand, the mail-order customer is often dealing with a company hundreds of miles away. Telephone calls are expensive and often difficult to arrange when the company has a post office box as its address and no listed telephone number for customers to call. It is not commonly known that a customer has the right to get the actual business address of a mail-order company. The postmaster of the city in which the box is located will supply it on request if you explain in writing why you want it.

Moreover, the ordinary complaint letter is often unavailing, prompting, when answered at all, form responses that evade even the appearance of remedial action. One such annoying form letter simply tells a customer clamoring for delivery of goods paid for months earlier that the company "has no record of the order." Other standard responses to complaints about undelivered mail orders are dodges intended to induce further writing. "Our records indicate that your order is being processed." "Our supplies were exhausted by the unusually heavy demand but we expect to be shipping your order shortly." "Your order has already been shipped."

In many cases the sums involved are significant but not sufficient to provoke legal action, especially when the satisfaction of any judgment would be problematic. "The unfilled mail order," declared the executive director of the Michigan Consumer's Council, "is a problem particularly aggravating to the aggrieved consumer because of his practical inability to deal, except by mail, with the seller in an attempt to resolve his complaint. The consumer who has paid money for undelivered mail-order goods or services, and confronts nothing but cold unresponsiveness or broken pledges from the distant seller finds himself with very little viable recourse."

The strict requirements of proof and the absence of subpoena power make prosecutions by the postal service under the postal criminal fraud statute, as well as civil administrative actions pursuant to the postal false representation statute, an ineffectual and sharply limited remedy. In addition, as most mail-order transactions occur in interstate commerce, remedial action on the state level is hampered by jurisdictional limitations. A state consumer protection official decried the same problem: "We at the intrastate level are virtually helpless in reaching the practices of the mail-order house operating from outside (the state)." The attorney general of West Virginia concurred: "In these cases, we face the same difficulty as do consumer protection agencies in most states—the selling firm is located outside our jurisdiction, and for all practical purposes is not accessible to us." Similarly, better business bureaus and chambers of commerce often can do no more than join the consumer in his/her letter-writing campaign.

You do, however, have certain rights and they can be upheld. You can also take some measures to ensure as much satisfaction for yourself as a mail-order customer as you receive when dealing with any other kind of company. The Federal Trade Commission has promulgated a rule (the Mail Order Merchandising Rule) designed to protect consumers who shop by mail. Under this rule the seller must ship your order no later than 30 days after receiving your order. If the seller does not ship when promised (or within 30 days if no delivery date has been promised), you have the right to cancel your order and get a prompt refund.

If the seller cannot meet the promised shipping date (or 30-day period), the seller must send you an "option notice," giving you a new shipment date and the option of accepting this new date or of canceling your order and getting a full, prompt refund. The seller must explain how to cancel your order with this notice and provide you with a cost-free way to reply. If you agree to the delayed shipping date (or do not respond), but the seller cannot meet the new date, the seller must send you a second option notice. You may accept the new delayed date by signing your consent on the second notice and returning it to the seller at the latter's expense or cancel your order and get a full, prompt refund. This time, however, if you do not respond at all, your order will be canceled automatically on the expiration of the first delay period and you are entitled to a full, prompt refund. More specifically, this means that if a prepaid order is canceled, the seller must mail your refund within seven business days. If you charged your purchase, the seller must adjust your account within one billing cycle.

There are exceptions to this rule. It does not apply to mail-order photo finishing; magazine subscriptions and other serial deliveries (except for the initial shipment); seeds and growing plants; C.O.D. orders; or credit orders where the account is not charged before the merchandise is shipped.

The rule also does not apply if you order by telephone and charge the order to your credit card or if your credit account is charged after the merchandise has been shipped. If you would prefer to be protected by this rule and have only the company's toll-free telephone number, you may call and ask for a mailing address to which you may send your order.

The Fair Credit Billing Act (a federal law) provides protection in limited circumstances if you are billed for a purchase by a credit card company. Under this law you have the same legal rights against the credit card issuer as you have against the company with which you are in dispute. Thus, if you would have the right to withhold payment from the mail-order company for undelivered or misrepresented goods, you also have the right to refuse to pay the credit card company.

However, this is a limited right. You must first try to resolve the matter with the seller. In addition, unless the card issuer owns or operates the seller's company, two other conditions must be met: the seller's company must be within 100 miles of your residence or within your home state; and the amount of the bill must exceed $50.

Most credit card companies will not insist that you comply with these technicalities so that, as a practical matter, it is relatively simple to interpose the credit card company between you and the vendor while you dispute the charge to your account. I once ordered a subscription to a newsletter and billed the $37 cost to a credit card. The vendor had apparently raised the price of the subscription to $48 in the time it had taken for my order to arrive. I thought the seller should have billed me at the lower price as per the order form, but that in any event I should have been given the option of deciding whether or not I wanted to pay the higher price.

One of the typical unsatisfactory ways such matters are handled is for the credit card company to forward your complaint to the vendor with a request to check the latter's records. The vendor then furnishes the credit card company with its billing slip (not your original order) indicating the higher price. The credit card company then forwards the billing slip indicating the higher price to you and disallows your claim, breezily adding that you should not hesitate to contact them again if they may be of further service. You are thus sent off to square one about two months after you sent in your original complaint, with the net result being that everybody has spun a few wheels without developing any traction.

If you then explain to the credit card company that the billing slip indicates a higher price than was printed on your order and ask it to request the original order form from the vendor, the latter no longer has it and it's already cost you, in time, effort and expense, more than the $11 you were trying to save. Back at the starting gate without credit for the overcharge, you have to decide whether to eat the overcharge, cancel the newsletter and demand a full refund or press on in an effort to get credit for the overcharge at further cost and expense when all you can expect to recover is the grand sum of $11.

You can easily finesse this kind of problem by photocopying all order forms you send through the mail and keeping them in a file folder or large envelope. Date your orders before photocopying them, so that if delivery isn't received within the time required by law, you will have easier recourse. If a problem later arises, simply retrieve the relevant copy from your file, make another copy of it for your own records and send one copy to the credit card company. The burden then shifts to the vendor. In the newsletter situation, for example, my account was credited with the overcharge by the time I received the next billing statement from the credit card company.

If you complain to your credit card company about a merchant that honored your card, always refer to it as "your vendor." "Vendor" is the term the credit card company uses in its own contracts with these establishments so it makes you sound more savvy if you use this word. The word "your" firms up the credit card company's responsibility for the problem, making it less likely it will impose the technical requirement that the amount involved be more than $50 or that the vendor be within 100 miles of your residence or within the same state.

You have probably received unordered merchandise in the

mail, with or without an accompanying bill. Subject to the exception noted below, unordered merchandise that comes to you via the United States mails is yours to keep as a gift. In fact, there are only two kinds of merchandise that may legally be sent to you without your consent: free samples, clearly labeled as such, and goods mailed by charities seeking contributions. These may also be kept as gifts, if unordered, and you may not be forced to pay for them or to return them. It is illegal for a seller to try to force you to return anything you did not order, or to bill you or dun you for payment. If you are billed for something that arrives through the mail unordered, I suggest you respond by asking the seller to supply proof that you placed the order. If the seller persists, see "carboning the western world," pp. 47–49.

If unordered merchandise comes to you, not through the mail, but via a private delivery service, you must do two things before you may lawfully keep the goods. First, you are required to tell the sender you received the unordered merchandise. Second, you need to give the sender a reasonable amount of time in which to pick up the goods at its own expense.

The exception to the unordered merchandise rule is the negative option plan. This is an agreement you, the buyer, make with a seller to the effect that, unless you inform the seller within a certain time period not to send the merchandise, you will receive it automatically and be billed for it. Book and record clubs often make use of a negative option plan. Buyers are usually given an introductory offer at a low price if they agree to buy a number of additional items on a negative option plan. Advertisers of such plans must disclose the terms of the plan, including: (1) how many items you are required to buy in a given period of time; (2) how often the company will send you offers; (3) whether you will be billed for shipping and handling; (4) how you may inform the seller if you do not want the item offered; and (5) your right to cancel your membership after fulfilling your obligation.

You must be given a minimum of ten days in which to notify the seller that you are declining a particular item offered. If you receive an item you don't want after having been given less than ten days in which to decline it, the Negative Option Rule requires the seller to take it back, pay the shipping cost for items returned and to give you full credit. Companies using negative option plans must also send a description of the product and a dated form you may return if you don't want it; ship any introductory or bonus merchandise within thirty days of receipt of your order; and not send any substitute merchandise without first obtaining your permission.

The United States Postal Service and the Federal Trade Commission Bureau of Consumer Protection have issued some guidelines for mail-order buyers. If you haven't heard of the company or it doesn't advertise a street address or a telephone number, check with your local consumer protection office, which may have a file on the seller or be willing to check further for you with a consumer protection office near the seller's mailing address. You may also want to check with the Better Business Bureau or the Direct Marketing Association (6 East 43 Street, New York, N.Y. 10017) or the Postal Inspection Service, with which your local post office can put you in touch.

Read the product description carefully. Don't rely on a photograph, which may make the product appear larger than it is. In one imaginative mail-order scam, the advertiser's offer involved a set of wicker furniture that was said to be "exactly as pictured." Although most buyers expected to receive porch or patio furniture that could seat themselves and their guests, the tiny, dollhouse variety that arrived was, indeed, the same size pictured in the ad.

Know what you're ordering. The copy can be as deceptive as the photograph. A mail-order company advertised a United States Government-approved steel engraving of George Washington. The product was a two-cent U.S. postage stamp. Medieval by comparison with contemporary mail-order scammery, variations of the same deceptive practice are still enriching some "hit and run" mail-order merchants.

Find out about the seller's return policy. If it isn't stated, ask before you order. You also have a right to get a copy of any warranty offer before you buy. When ordering, complete the order form as directed. If it is not complete, your order may be delayed. The delivery time promised in the ad (or the 30-day period if no time is specified), does not begin until the seller receives a properly completed order.

Get a clear idea of the value of the item you are considering buying by direct marketing by comparison shopping. Be aware of who pays handling and shipping costs. They can sometimes be enough to counterbalance or neutralize what you thought was a bargain.

Some companies reserve the right to substitute a comparable product if they don't have on hand what you order. If you don't want a substitute, be sure to state "No substitutes" on the order form.

Never send cash through the mails. In addition to the possibility of theft or loss, you will have no proof of payment if a dispute arises. A canceled check, money order receipt or credit card statement is written proof of payment.

Keep a photocopy of the order form you send. If you are responding to a catalog, magazine or newspaper offer, or one you receive in the mail, keep the advertisement. Be sure you have the seller's name and address and the date you mailed your order. If the advertisement appeared in a magazine or newspaper, note the name and date. If you respond to a radio or television offer, keep a record of the station, date and time the offer was broadcast. These simple precautions don't take much time or effort and they pay dividends if something goes awry.

Most of your mail orders will be routine. You will usually get about what you pay for, and sometimes you may even be delightfully surprised, as I have, with a unique item that isn't overpriced and will probably last a hundred years. However, some surprises that arrive by mail (or fail ever to arrive) are not so delightful. On these infrequent occasions, it's comforting to know that you don't simply have to write it off, that you can reach out across the country and flip the situation about decisively, even with the less tractable mail-order merchants who do their preying Monday through Friday.

If you have a complaint against a mail-order company with which you are not familiar, I suggest that you depart from the usual practice and contact top management early on. One of the reasons you may never have heard of the company is that it hasn't been in business long, nor does it intend to stay in business under that name much longer. It will go bankrupt or suspend operations when sufficient complaints pile up, only to reappear under a new name on the same premises or perhaps somewhere else, under the same management, all in an effort to stay two jumps ahead of the law.

It's therefore important to move quickly and the telephone is the recommended route. The ordinary mailed complaint can be ignored or you can be given deliberately vague answers that deny relief indefinitely. For fast action when you are dealing with a company that has furnished only a post office box number, you can get the actual business address of the company by requesting it from the postmaster of the city in which the box is located.

You can do even better. You can usually get the names

and home addresses of top management by requesting this information from the secretary of state at the state capital in which the post office box is located. I once had occasion to call the president of a mail-order company during the dinner hour (his, not mine). I met his truculent élan with a terse, calm recitation of the facts about an undelivered item and the legal consequences of further inaction and requested an immediate refund. The company's remittance arrived in short order, postmarked the next day.

Top management of mail-order companies are more sensitive to jeopardy than are lower-level personnel. Some of the latter are fairly low-paid, have no great love for the company or its management and are not highly motivated to remove the company from harm's way by giving you what you want. Many others simply don't have the authority to make you whole.

In a case in point, I once bought some collector plates in response to a direct-mail solicitation. My thought was to buy four sets, sell two later at double the purchase price, taking me out of the total cost of the four sets, and to hold the other two sets for further appreciation. The venture was not motivated by a desire to appreciate fine art (which these plates were not) at close range; it was a simple quest for profit.

A couple of years later, I received a price list from the same company. The plates had advanced smartly and were then selling at about double what I'd paid. I mailed in orders to sell two sets as originally planned. The orders were to remain in effect until the plates were sold unless I later canceled them before such a sale took place. Several months later, another price list from the company quoted even higher prices for my plates but mine had apparently never been sold. I called the company's toll-free number for an explanation.

They had computerized their trading operation, I was

told. All orders had been canceled in the process. If I still wanted to sell my plates, I would have to reenter my orders. What was the current quote on the plates? "Well, at the moment," I was informed, "there was no bid for most of them." My attempts at further discussion brought repetition of what they'd done and what I would "have to do," but no progress. It was clear, by the way this person continued to repeat the company's policy, that he lacked authority to give me what I wanted. I had the call transferred.

The vice president in charge of trading sounded like an intelligent, charming woman. When she repeated the fact that they'd canceled all the orders on their books when they computerized their trading operation, my response was simple and doubtless less charming. "When I mailed in open orders they were to remain in effect until the items were sold unless I canceled them. The company didn't have the right to cancel these orders without notice. I wasn't even informed of this arbitrary decision. Look here," I said, reaching for my "key ring" of handy words and phrases, "I'm not alleging mail fraud, but if the company's price lists are legitimate, I am entitled to have sold two sets of these plates, as ordered. If you assume it was only the company's negligence, not fraud, that prevented this sale, I'm still entitled to have sold two sets."

"Let me check our records and I'll see what can be done."

Raising the ante, I replied, "I have four sets of these plates and I'd like to sell all of them at the prices on my orders. I'm entitled to have sold only two sets but I'd like to sell all of them. Please confirm the sale of the two sets and let me know about one or both of the other two sets."

This vice president returned the call a short time later. The company was willing to give me $313.60 for each of two sets but would not bid for the other two sets at the moment. This was an entirely reasonable offer and I accepted it. Each set had cost about $150. I sent the plates by insured mail and received their check for $627.20 shortly thereafter.

"I'm not alleging mail fraud," is a serviceable response to a mail-order seller trying to evade its responsibilities. The words "mail fraud" are about as welcome to a mail-order company as "salmonella" to a food processor or "boll weevils" to a cotton farmer. "Mail fraud" conjures the burden of opposing a relentless governmental force with lots of paperwork and high risk. The word "alleging" gave a legal emphasis to the sentence, a little verbal English or spin, adding to the image of high costs (lawyers defending companies bill for their services) and it added credibility to the speaker by being "of a piece." "Alleging" and "mail fraud" are both legal terms. They resonate together in the listener's ear. Finally, the word "not" implies a way out, a means of avoiding the confrontation or clash.

I mentioned "carboning the western world" earlier. If your initial attempt to resolve your legitimate complaint doesn't bring satisfaction, this technique is a good equalizer. It applies leverage to the company and helps it decide to do what's right—i.e., satisfy you. Carboning the western world raises the ante for the company from the mere bad will of a disappointed customer (which the company has already found it easy to disregard) to a point where it may be less costly to give you your due. Include in your "cc" notation to the extreme left of your signature your local postmaster and that of the company, your local and state consumer protection office and that of the company, the Chief Postal Inspector, U.S. Postal Service, Washington, D.C. 20260-2161, the magazine, newspaper or radio or television station that carried the advertisement, the Direct Marketing Association, 6 East 43 Street, New York, N.Y. 10017, the Federal

Trade Commission, Washington, D.C. 20580, your state attorney general and that of the company, and your local BBB and that of the company.

You will get best and fastest results by bringing all of this outside pressure (and the looming threat of repercussions, unforeseen consequences and lots of paperwork) to bear at one time and as quickly as possible after the company fails to make good or attempts to put you on hold. However, if you want to spare the expense of postage and photocopying, you may send only the original letter with the "cc" list at the bottom and a postscript to the company to the effect that you are giving the company a last opportunity to make good but that if it doesn't, you will send the copies in ten days. If asked to return the goods, get a receipt from the shipper.

Junk mail is a problem for some people. Your name and address almost undoubtedly appear on a number of mailing lists. List brokers rent and sell these names and addresses and before long you receive a proliferation of direct-mail solicitations that include several "life-changing" offers. If you'd like to restrict this flow, a card or letter to the Direct Marketing Association, 6 East 43 Street, New York, N.Y. 10017-4609 will get you delisted by their member companies and spare you from about one half to two thirds of this paper onslaught. For those who would prefer to be kept informed of what's available, the DMA will be happy to have your name and address added to its members' lists.

☐ How to Be Your Own Best Friend

As you experience the benefits and joys that result from filtering out of your life marketplace losses, waste and frustrations and learn to convert the occasional nonsense that somehow evades filtration to satisfactory resolutions, you are likely to discover new techniques or refinements that play into your own special abilities and strengths. Your success in creating desired effects will encourage repetition of the successful activity and experimentation with it. This, in turn, will introduce variations to which you will react, producing innovation, creativity, growth and power.

This active approach will spill over into other areas of your life and take you beyond previous limitations, adding texture and breadth to the fabric of your life. Like any other successful person, you will not limit yourself to the status quo. No box can hold you or define you or keep you immobilized. Creative changes are based on activity.

If you are willing to be venturesome, to go beyond the four corners of what is prescribed for you, you can enter into a creative interaction with life and open up myriad opportunities. You need not simply follow patterns preset and premeasured for you by somebody else. You can remove the limitations on your life with your own hands. You can develop your own alternate routes to success in whatever you undertake. If you are willing to experiment, to take detours in the continuation of the journey, to find other vehicles, who can stop you from arriving at your destination despite unforeseen obstacles?

Sensible people don't keep pressing the same lever that doesn't yield the desired result. Paradoxically, the most successful people don't keep pressing the same lever even if it does provide their objective because they know that reliance on one particular lever soon becomes a dependency that inhibits personal growth and development. If you have the courage to dare to succeed, you will keep inventing new ways to go forward. Expand your possibilities and you own, in yourself, an equity machine. You cease to be merely a hired hand and become the owner of the franchise. Which cards you play, in what order, with whom and when are matters of your own personal style. The willingness to play is even more fundamental than the desire to win.

In our society, which is blessedly free and open, the so-called givens are not immutable. They may be challenged and changed with surprising ease through your own efforts. Those who adopt a rigid, all-or-nothing view of life sentence themselves to a series of Procrustean outcomes. As a result, they experience life as a series of deprivations. In silent sorrow, they watch others smoothly interact with their environment, custom tailoring results and rewards to their needs and desires.

By a single act of will you can decide to pick and choose, as at a smorgasbord. You may make ethical choices without the necessity to "take it all" or to "leave it all." Once this decision is taken, you are en route to the active approach to living that makes life infinitely richer and more pleasurable by creating undreamed-of new possibilities within your ability to conceive and obtain.

In these pages I have set down the methods and techniques that have brought excellent results for me and others. This approach is soundly and broadly based on the ways people think and act in the real world. Suppose, however, that some new element were added to the water supply or some new mode of thinking were so widely disseminated that people began to think and act somewhat differently. If that happened, the methods and techniques I've been using successfully for years might become less reliable. What then?

Those who were unable to adjust to changed and changing conditions would find themselves less well able to cope tomorrow with yesterday's rules, even as the application of such rules learned as children and still adhered to so rigidly by the aging child who mastered them long ago leaves many bewildered and unsatisfied. None of this material will give you the benefits and satisfactions you deserve unless you use it creatively in the world as you find and engage it. This material is best viewed, not as a vocabulary, but as a grammar, for which you will supply many elements of vocabulary to meet a variety of situations. This material is meant, not as a textbook, but as a workbook; not as an end product, but as a work in progress.

The most difficult wounds to heal are self-inflicted and, unfortunately, they are subject to relapse unless the will and the spirit are working positively and harmoniously. Self-imposed limitations are the most insidious. In the context of resolving marketplace disputes to your satisfaction, there are many ways to obtain a good result and only one certain way to fail: namely, to take yourself out of the game, to lose heart, to give up.

In these pages I've described all of the methods and techniques I've used to turn justified complaints with a host of sellers over the past twenty years into happy endings. It's all here, as of this writing. Nothing has been held back. Others may introduce stylistic differences in executing any of these plays but this is my entire playbook, committed to paper in a workable system for the first time.

When to call the plays and how to run them, in what order, with what degree of intensity, with how much perseverance, the particular timing of the moves to be made, your own credibility and personality, all of these factors will make your playing of any particular hand uniquely your own. However, with practice, the level of your game will improve and you will develop a better ear, a surer touch, in handling these matters for yourself. Your will and your spirit, an openness to experimentation, a sense of propriety and a purity of heart will animate and authenticate every move you make. Movement is the antidote to stagnation, hopelessness and powerlessness. If you decide to suit up and get into this game, my hope is that you will discover better plays than I have and achieve every success you desire.

In India, the workhorse of the society is the elephant. Before a young elephant is pressed into service, it is placed in a clearing and a chain is shackled about one of its legs by a peg driven through two links into the ground. The young elephant cannot remove the peg and learns to accept it.

Years later, when the fully grown elephant is able to uproot trees with its prodigious strength, it is anchored by a similar, somewhat larger, chain about one of its legs and a similar peg. The elephant is no longer unable to remove the peg yet it remains anchored, not by any present disability but by past failures.

□ INDEX

Agencies. *See* Consumer agencies
Airline travel, 144–47, 154–55, 159
  available fares, examples of,
    146–47
  comparison shopping and, 146
  complaints, 160–61
  major-airport concept, 145–46
  overbookings and, 155, 159
  personal computers and, 153
  special fares, 154–55
  two cross-country round trips for
    price of one, 145
  See also Travel agents
Air Travelers' Fly Rights, 159
American Association for Retired
  People, 154
American Bar Association, 123
American Institute of Architects,
  200
American Medical Association,
  129–30
American Society of Travel Agents
  (ASTA), 156–57
Architect(s), 188–95
  -client relationship, 191, 192
  collaborative efforts and, 194
  consultation fees, 191–92
  cost-free inquiries about, 190

general contractors and, 191
  initial meeting with, 192–93
  overall renovation plan and,
    188–89
  piecemeal jobs, 194
  plan and finances, 189
  references from former clients of,
    191
  second meeting with, 193
  selecting, 189–94
  written agreement with, 194–96
  See also General contractors;
    Home improvements
Attorneys. *See* Lawyers
Authorities. *See* Company
  authorities
Automobile sales. *See* Car sales
Auto Safety Hotline, 224

Bandler, Richard, 49
Barron's, 179
Better Business Bureau, 236
"Blue Book," 208, 222

"Carboning the western world,"
  55–57, 241
Car sales, 205–25
  "Blue Book" for, 208

car loans, 208
"closers" or sales managers,
    216–17
as complex transaction, 209–10
computer printout service for
    data on, 206–7
contracts for, 220–21
"corporate twins" and, 207–8
credit terms, 217–19
"dealer prep" costs, 214
dealer's cost for car, 207, 215–16
delivery date, 220–21
financing the purchase, 208,
    217–18
information for consumers, 206
making a fixed offer, 210–11
money spent on, 205
monthly payments, 217–18
options and, 214–15
"ready-to-buy-today" approach,
    210–11
salespersons and, 205–6
showroom visits, 208–9
stereo systems, factory-installed,
    214
test drives, 213–14
trade-ins and, 211–13, 215
See also Used car sales
Chief Postal Inspector, 241
Choice, 19–21
benefit of doubt for seller, 20
flagrant cases and, 21
minor wrongs and, 20
personal risk and, 20–21
size and scale of transaction as
    criteria, 21
when to complain, 19–21
Civil Aeronautics Board (CAB),
    159
Company authorities, 25–32
allowing for appeals to higher
    authorities, 27
chief executives, 26
factors prohibiting full remedy,
    32
initiating a complaint, 26–27

middle management, 31
"non-helpers," avoiding, 27
reaching the right person, 25
routine procedures and, 26
telephone tactics, 27–32
See also Top level management
Consumer agencies, 78–84
collaborative effort with, 80
departments of consumer affairs,
    80–84
licensing bodies, 79–80
"parrot case," 83–84
regulatory agencies, 79
shirt damaged at laundry, case
    example, 81–83
skill in soliciting help, 80
small claims court and, 78
typing service and, case example,
    82–83
Consumer complaints:
airline travel and, 144–47,
    154–55
architects and, 188–95
car sales and, 205–25
choices about, 19–21
company authorities and, 25–32
consumer agencies and, 78–84
contracts and, 74–77
corporate headquarters and, 64–68
discovering new techniques for,
    243–44
distinguishing one's case, 47–50
documentation for, 58–63
expectations and, 22–24
general contractors and, 195–204
gratuities and gifts and, 85–91
health care and, 127–43
home improvements and,
    185–204
hospitalization and surgery and,
    138–43
hotels and, 147–64
insurance claim, case example,
    22–24
lawyers and, 101–26
letters of complaint, 54–57

mail order businesses and,
226–42
minor wrongs and, 20
palatable objectives in, 51–53
personal risk and, 20–21
promotions, self-nomination for,
75–77
reasonableness and, 92–97
salary review and, 75–77
self-imposed limitations and, 245
small claims court and, 78
stockbrokers and, 165–84
telephone tactics, 27–32, 34,
38–41
time considerations and, 69–73
top level management and,
33–37
travel agents and, 155–59
used car sales and, 221–25
vocabulary and, 42–46
when to complain, 19–21
Consumer Reports, 206
*Consumer Reports Annual Auto
Issue,* 207
*Consumer Reports Guide to Used
Cars,* 221–22
Consumers Union, 206
Contingent fees, 118–19
Contracts, 74–77
for insurance, 75
promotions, self-nomination for,
75–77
salary reviews, 75
standard forms, 74
Corporate headquarters, 64–68
assistants or executive
secretaries, 66
best approach to, 67
insecurity among executives in
subsidiary, 66
legal department, asking for, 67
name-dropping tactic, 66
toll-free number for, 67
understatement as tool at, 67
Cunningham, Glenn, 96

Delivery dates, 70
Departments of consumer affairs,
80–84
See also Consumer agencies
Direct Marketing Association
(DMA), 227, 236, 241
Discount brokers, 178, 179
*Discount Guide for Travelers Over
55, The* (Wentz and
Wentz), 154
Distinguishing one's case, 47–50
company policy, attacks on,
48–49
dramatizing specifics of case,
49–50
house rules and, 47–48
stating objective as need, 49
"word salad" and, 49
Doctors. *See* Health care;
Hospitalization and surgery
Documentation, 58–63
canceled checks, 59
credit-card receipts, 59
files for, 58
names of people involved, 59
photographs as, 60–61
Rolodex files for, 58–59
ten-year storage of, 59
written records of transactions,
59
Drug Evaluations, 129

Expectations, 22–24
high level of, 22
insurance claim, case example,
22–24
objectives, advance decisions
about, 24

Fair Credit Billing Act, 232–33
Federal Register, 228
Federal Trade Commission, 227,
228–29, 241–42
Frogs into Princes (Bandler and
Grinder), 49

General contractors, 191, 195–204
architects and, 191, 196
contracts with, 200
cost-plus contracts, 201–2
decision to hire, 195–96
as director of one's project,
202–3
elderly homeowners and (fraud
case), 196–97
estimates of total costs by,
199–200
financing of project and, 203
fixed-fee contracts with, 202
former clients of, checking on,
199
fraud by, 196–98
guarantees and warranties in
contracts, 201, 203
holding back final percentage of
fee, 203
importance of, 202
inspection by local building
inspector, 203–4
itemized statement of work done
by, 203
licensing and, 199
local agencies as sources for,
198–99
payment schedule and, 200
penalty for slow work by, 200
recommended by knowledgeable
people, 198–99
remodeled kitchen (fraud case),
197–98
selecting, 198–200
See also Architects; Home
improvements
Gifts. See Gratuities and gifts
Goldinger, Shirley, 196
Gratuities and gifts, 85–91, 141
annual or seasonal, 90
children traveling alone and, 90
hospitals and, 141
parking garage attendants and,
85, 88–89
in restaurants, 86–88, 89
verbal expression of appreciation
vs., 90–91
Grinder, John, 49
Guinness Book of World Records,
The, 9, 96

H. A. L. T. (Help Abolish Legal
Tyranny), 124–25
Health care, 127–43
appointments made by third
party, 134–35
author's case with thyroid,
131–32
author's experience with
nose-throat specialist,
136–37
complacency of patients, 128
consumer tactics, 132–38
diagnostic testing, inconclusivity
of, 130–31
disadvantages of patient role,
127–28
doctor-patient relationship,
137–38
drugs, overprescription of, 129
hospital affiliation of doctor, 137
learning about diagnosed
condition, 131
list of questions for doctor, 135
Physicians' Desk Reference
(PDR), patient's use of, 129
recommendations for doctor by
other professionals, 138
reducing doctor's bill by
patient's waiting time in
office, 133–34
second opinions, 131
selecting a doctor, 137–38
third party presence at
consultation, 135
time spent by patient in doctor's
waiting office, 132–34
Home improvements, 185–204
architects and. See Architect(s)
general contractors and. See
General contractors

general discussion of, 185–88
renovation and planning, 188
sales pitches for, rejecting,
185–86
scams, 186–87
Hospitalization and surgery, 138–43
documents signed by patients,
143
food at hospitals, 142–43
gratuities and gifts, 141
hospital as "expensive hotel,"
141
insurance coverage, 138–40
nursing care and, 139–40
patients' rights and, 143
semiprivate room charges, 140
VIP treatment, how to secure,
140–43
Hotels, 147–64
author's experience at Caribbean
hotel, 161–63
complaints about service, 161
convention and tourist bureaus,
153
corporate rate for, 147–49
discount cards for, 151–53
"How to Survive a Hotel Fire"
and, 164
overbooking rip-off by, 157–59
overbookings at, 155
quiet rooms at, how to secure,
149–51
senior citizen discounts and, 154
weekend packages and, 153
"House rules." *See* Rules of the
company
*How I Turn Ordinary Complaints
into Thousands of Dollars*
(Charell), 9
How to Get the Upper Hand
(Charell), 10, 11–12, 13, 34
"How to Survive a Hotel Fire," 164

"Iatrogenic," defined, 127
IBEW (International Brotherhood
of Electrical Workers), 196

Inflation and services, 14–15
Institute of Certified Travel Agents
(ICTA), 157
Insurance claim case, 22–24
high initial offer and, 22
inflated claims and, 22
settlement price, when to state,
23–24
Insurance contracts, 75

Junk mail, 242

Lawyers, 101–26
advertising by, 109
agreement to try case personally,
120
automobile accident case and,
102–5
bar committee chairpersons, 112
breach of contract, grounds for,
121
clients' relationship with, 115
comparison shopping for, 109
conflict of interest and, 120–21
contingent fees and, 118–19
early hiring of, 108
fees, 116–19, 123–24
files kept by client, 125
firing of, 126
flat fees and, 117
governmental agencies as helpful
legal source, 106–7
hourly billings, 122–23
inadequate preparation by, 104
information as real need, 106
initial meeting with, 114–16
introductory fee for meeting,
114
law school professors,
recommendations from,
111–12
legal clinics and, 109
legal directories, 110, 113
minimum fees, 116
need for, establishing, 106, 107–8
"negligence," 103

overbilling, complaint tactics for, 124–26
overmatched by opposing side, 104–5
percentage basis fees, 118
preparation, signs of, 115
questions to ask about, 105
"reasonable fee provision" and, 124–25
recommendations by businessmen and professionals, 112
referral services and, 110
research law libraries, client's use of, 107
retainer agreements and, 103
right lawyer for right job, 108
safeguards against incompetence, lack of, 101
screening of, 113
second opinions by, 102
selection of, 108–113
solo practitioners vs. law firms, 110–11
time costs, 121–23
working law libraries, client's use of, 107
written agreement with, 117–18
Lawyers' Code of Professional Responsibility, 124
Legal clinics, 109
Legal services. *See* Lawyers
Letters of complaint, 54–57
admission of fault and, 54
"brown paper bag" letters, 55
"carboning the western world," 55–57
criticism of employees and, 54
expensive stationery and, 55
one-page limit for, 54
presentation as profit opportunity, 54–55
Lewolt, Dan, 124
Licensing bodies, 79–80
See also Consumer agencies

Mail order businesses, 226–42
author's experience with collector plates, 239–41
"carboning the western world" and 241
credit card orders, 232–34
Fair Credit Billing Act and, 232–33
Federal Trade Commission study on, 227, 228–29
form-letter responses to complaints against, 230
guidelines for customers of, 236
history of, 226–27
insignificant sums and legal action, 230
as interstate commerce, 231
junk mail and, 242
Mail Order Merchandising Rule and, 231
as major source of all consumer complaints, 227–28
negative option plan of, 235–36
payment methods for, 237
photocopying all order forms, 234, 237
postal service, prosecutions by, 231
product descriptions, careful reading of, 236–37
refunds, difficulty in obtaining, 229
resolving complaints, difficulties in, 229–30
return policies of, 237
sales figures on, 226
shipping dates, 231–32
substitute merchandise sent by, 237
success of, reasons for, 227
telephone calls to, 230, 238
top management, contacting, 238–39
unordered merchandise from, 234–36
"vendor," defined, 234

Mail Order Merchandising Rule, 231
Management. *See* Company
  authorities; Top level
  management
Market mechanism, 14
Martindale-Hubbell (legal
  directory), 113
Medical professions. *See* Health
  care; Hospitalization and
  surgery
"Mr. Big." *See* Top level
  management

Name-dropping techniques, 35, 43,
  66
*National Automobile Dealers
  Association Official Used Car
  Guide* ("Blue Book"), 208,
  222
National Institute for Automotive
  Service Excellence (NIASE),
  224
National Safety Council, The, 164
Negative option plan, defined,
  235–36

"Omit charges," 39
Open stop orders, 184
Overbooking rip-off by hotels,
  157–59

Palatable objectives, 51–53
  cost-free items and, 51
  noisy hotel accommodations and,
    52–53
  seller's tendency to devalue stock
    items and, 52
  settlement costs at acceptable
    levels, 52
  unused capacity and, 51–52
Photographic documentation,
  60–61
  accidents and, 61
  parking tickets and, 61–62
  real estate and, 61
  in restaurants, 61, 62–63

Physicians' Desk Reference (PDR),
  129
Promotions, self-nomination for,
  75–77
  explaining one's position, 77
  requesting a meeting, 76–77
  salary reviews and, 75
  timing and, 76
  written preparation for, 76

Reasonableness and complaints,
  92–97
  abusing power, 93
  antisocial practices and, 95
  avoidance and prevention and,
    96
  conviction and, 95
  fairness, 94
  minimal force levels, 93
  personal attacks, 93–94
  "Regulations prohibiting" as useful
    phrase, 40
Regulatory agencies, 79
  See also Consumer agencies
Restaurant service:
  dinner reservations, 86
  gratuities and, 86–88, 89
  photographic documentation
    and, 61, 62–63
Rosenthal, Benjamin, 229
Rules of the Company, 47–48
  inherently bad rules, 47
  reasonable rules affecting
    customer disproportionately,
    48
  reasonable rules unreasonably
    applied, 47–48

Salary review, 75
  See also Promotions,
    self-nomination for
Senior citizen discounts, 154
Services:
  consumer protection and, 11–12
  evaluation of, 12
  inflation and, 14–15

information on protection, 13
market mechanism and, 14
price guideposts, absence of, 12
rating systems for, lack of, 12
U. S. economy and, 11
Shapiro, Esther K., 197, 198
Small claims court, 78
Stockbrokers, 165–84
"broker of the day," 177–78
confirmation slips and, 175–76
contracts with, 182–83
debit balance and, 181–82
discount brokers, 178, 179
discount commission rates,
179–81
emotional involvement of, 177
functioning as dealers, 175
honesty of brokerage house and,
176
hot-tip scam, variations on,
167–70
"inside information," 166–70
items of value provided by, 182
losses, limiting, 184
margin debt, lowering interest
rate on, 181–82
misquotations scam and, 170–
72
negligence liability of, 182–83
negotiability of commissions,
179–81
"not-so-special special situation"
and, 173–74
opening a second account, 182
performance as guide to, 183–84
pressure upon customer to trade,
165
letting profits run, 184
recommendations from
professionals about, 176
romantic stories about stocks by,
174–76
secondary distribution of large
holdings and, 173–74
selecting, 176
testing, 172
visiting recommended firms, 177

Telephone Tactics, 27–32, 34, 38–41
best person to help, asking for,
30–31
brevity of calls, 30
chief operator (or supervisor),
dealing with, 29–30
clear objectives and, 40
engraved-stationery, case
example, 39
identifying oneself, 29
names, asking for, 28, 29–30
person-to-person calls, 34
"poor me" complaints, 41
"reading" character and, 27
"regulations prohibiting" as
useful phrase, 40
simple presentations, 41
unsatisfactory answers and, 28
Time considerations, 69–73
control over, 71
delivery dates, 70
"larks and owls" concept, 72–73
negotiability of time
commitments, 71–72
prime and fringe time, 72
reservations for dinner and, 70
at standard rates, 72–73
Tipping. See Gratuities and gifts
Top level management, 33–37
barrier-breaking techniques,
33–36
difficulty reaching, 33
leaving one's telephone number,
35
name-dropping tactic, 35
person-to-person calls, 34
"runarounds," mentioning, 36
Travel agents, 155–59
bargains and, 156
as buffer and lever for service
complaints, 163–64
overbooking rip-offs and, 157–59
overbookings and, 155
professional associations of,
156–57
quantity discounts and, 156
questions to ask, 157

Travel services. *See* Airline travel; Hotels; Travel agents

United States Tour Operator's Association, 157
Used car sales, 221–25
  car rental agencies and, 223–24
  depreciation and, 221
  information on, 221
  inspection by auto mechanic, 224
  known safety hazards and, 224–25
  new-car dealers and, 223
  private sales, 222–23
  sources for, 222–24
  test drives, 224
  used-car dealers, 223
  vehicle identification number, checking, 224
  warranties and, 223, 224
  See also Car sales

Valentino, Rudolph, 92
Veterinarian, complaint case concerning, 44–45

Vocabulary for complaints, 42–46
  "doctor," invocation of, 43–44
  emotionally charged words and phrases, 42
  "in all fairness," 46
  "I need your help," 46
  "lawyer," invocation of, 43
  name-dropping tactic, 43
  veterinarian, case concerning, 44–45
  "would it be possible?," 46

Waiters and gratuities, 87–88
Walker, Gary, 83
Wentz, Caroline, 154
Wentz, Walter, 154
"Word salad," 49
Written complaints. *See* Letters of complaint

Zoroaster, 91

ABOUT THE AUTHOR

Ralph Charell has been knighted by the Mark Twain Society for his "outstanding contribution to American humor" and is recognized by *The Guinness Book of World Records* as "the world's most successful complainer." A former chief executive and operating officer of his own Wall Street securities firm and a former network television program executive, Charell has written two previous national best-sellers on this subject, *How I Turn Ordinary Complaints into Thousands of Dollars* and *How to Get the Upper Hand.* He holds a Juris Doctor from Columbia Law School and a Master of Fine Arts in Film, Radio and Television from Columbia University School of the Arts.